D0467478

A Christmas Filled with Miracles

A CHRISTMAS FILLED WITH MIRACLES

INSPIRING STORIES FOR THE MAGIC OF THE SEASON

MARY ELLEN

MJF BOOKS
NEW YORK

Published by MJF Books
Fine Communications
Two Lincoln Square
60 West 66th Street
New York, NY 10023

A Christmas Filled with Miracles
Library of Congress Catalog Card Number 2001090534
ISBN 1-56731-467-8

Copyright © 2000 by Mary Ellen Angelscribe

Book Design: Claudia Smelser
Author photo: Michael Sergason/Heritage Studio

Published by arrangement with Conari Press.

Manufactured in the United States of America on acid-free paper

MJF Books and the MJF colophon are trademarks of Fine Creative
Media, Inc.

10 9 8 7 6 5 4 3 2 1

This book is dedicated to you,
the Earth Angels
around the world
who create magic and miracles in others' lives.

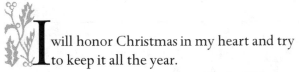

I will honor Christmas in my heart and try to keep it all the year.

—*Charles Dickens*

There are two ways to live your life. One is as though nothing is a miracle, the other is as though everything is a miracle.

—*Albert Einstein*

Never doubt that a small group of thoughtful, committed citizens can change the world; indeed, it's the only thing that ever has.

—*Margaret Mead*

You may only be one person to the world, but you may also be the world to one person.

—*Anonymous*

A Christmas Filled with Miracles

xii

Foreword

by Doreen Virtue, Ph.D.,
author of Divine Guidance *and* Angel Therapy

REMEMBER WHEN YOU were a child on Christmas morning? If you're like me, you woke up early, excited about the promise that the day held. My little brother and I would softly tiptoe into the living room, holding our breath so as not to wake our parents. Our eyes would survey the beautiful display of packages that had magically appeared beneath the Christmas tree. We'd shake the presents, trying to guess their contents.

Many years later, after my parents had "the talk" with me about Santa Claus, Christmas took on a different type of magic. It was then that I truly felt my parents' love being expressed through presents. There was the Christmas following my dad's transition from the corporate world to self-employment. Money was tight, and it looked like I wouldn't receive that ten-speed bike I hankered for. But when we returned from a Christmas Eve family outing, I entered the house and gasped when I saw my shiny new bike, sporting a large red bow, next to the tree.

On another memorable Christmas, I received an exquisite porcelain model horse. Oohing and ahhing over its delicate features, I accidentally knocked it over, shattering its left ear. I was devastated, but my father calmly took the little Arabian horse into his office. Dad lovingly rebuilt the ear from a special clay, even painting it to match the other ear. At that moment, the magic of Christmas transitioned from believing that a mysterious red-suited man dropped presents from a sleigh to understanding that love was the greatest gift of all.

You probably also have favorite memories of Christmas gatherings and gifts. Some of your memories may seem bittersweet, because they revolve around family members who have now passed into heaven. Other memories may involve wishes that came true or times when you enjoyed giving joy to others. And you may have memories of Christmases that were truly miraculous, involving God's Earth Angels and heavenly Angels alike.

In this book, you'll read about such miracles. Here are remarkable stories to fill your heart year-round with the love and the magic that is Christmas. Just when you feel overwhelmed by shopping-mall Santas and too much commercialism, this book is a refreshing glass of Christmas cheer.

These stories inspire us all to become Earth Angels ourselves. And perhaps there is no better time to practice getting our wings than during the holiday season. For, during the stressful shopping hours and family gatherings, when we take the time to hold open a door for a stranger, to sincerely thank a helpful clerk, or to donate toys to needy families, we receive the greatest gift we can give to ourselves and the world: the embodiment of love, which is the true spirit of Christmas.

The original Christmas story is a miraculous tale. We've all read about the Angels, the Virgin Birth, and the guiding light of the Star. But miracles didn't disappear from Earth 2,000 years ago. They still occur daily, to people just like you and me. Probably you've experienced a miracle or two yourself. The stories that you're about to read can recharge our spiritual batteries and remind us all of the importance of kindness and the reality of miracles, especially during the holiday season. My prayer is that by reading this book, you'll rekindle some of that wondrous anticipation that you may have felt as a child on Christmas morning. And with that spirit of faith, you'll expect miracles . . . and receive them . . . at Christmas and always.

Hope and Inspiration
Are the Music of the Soul

An Act of Kindness,
When wrapped in love,
Is often the ingredient
That creates miracles for others.

Mary Ellen Angelscribe

HAVE YOU NOTICED when people are kind, miracles happen? And when people are open and willing to be a Divine Vehicle for God's love and they offer to the world kind words, thoughts, and deeds, they create miracles for themselves and for others?

I am a housewife who was motivated to share with others the good news and the miracles that were taking place in my family's life. I had no idea what was about to unfold when I started sharing my stories with friends. I sent the stories out on the Internet, and, in just a matter of weeks, they had circulated around the world, one person passing them on to the next. In response to this interest, I started an Internet newsletter titled the *Angels and Miracles Good-News-Letter,* that was available free to anyone who wanted to receive it (www. angelscribe. com/subscribe.html). In three years, more than 50,000 readers were reading the newsletter. Five years have now gone by, and what started as a passion for me has developed into a blessing for many, as more and more people have shared their own miraculous stories.

I want to make a positive difference in the world, and the Internet newsletter has become my volunteer act of kindness, my little something to make the world a better and brighter place. I believe that each of us has the power to do good things within our center of influence. All the events we encounter in our lives, on our daily paths, create our destiny designed by God.

In a moment of overwhelm, after receiving literally hundreds of e-mails with miracle stories for the newsletter, I lightly complained in the newsletter that I had no idea why the media focused on so much negative news when the world was brimming with more good news and miracles than I could possibly share! Brenda Knight, at Conari Press in California, had heard about the *Angels and Miracles Good-News-Letter* through Jeff Rogers, one of Conari's Random Acts of Kindness™ volunteers in Hawaii. Brenda had been reading the newsletters he had forwarded to her, and, after reading my "complaint," she phoned to say that Conari would love to do a book on miracles. A number of conversations with the people at Conari Press followed; the result was a book on miracles titled *Expect Miracles.*

A book on miracles is truly created on the wings of heaven. *Expect Miracles* was surrounded with miracles while we were putting the book together and after it was published. As I was editing the stories and deciding which ones would be heartwarming and good teachers of God's love in action, I began to feel nervous. Here I was, a housewife who had no writing, editing, media, or college training, and I was in the process of creating a book already scheduled for publication. My nervousness grew with my realization that *Expect Miracles* was not going to be an ordinary book, and the likelihood of it being featured in the media became clear. I had a fear of public speaking and the possibility of radio and television talk show appearances made me anxious. Would I be up to the pressures?

One Tuesday afternoon, as my fears continued to grow, I turned off the computer, went to the kitchen, gazed out the window, and spoke to God/Spirit/the Angels. I know we attract what we fear and that fear holds us back from our destiny of happiness. I prayed, "Dear God, if you bring me media opportunities to do your work, I promise to show up. I promise to set my fears aside and do what is brought to me. But, Dear God, here is the deal: Please, please do not let my mind go blank!" I asked God and the Angels for their comfort and for the right things to say. I spoke to them in my heart and said that if they guided me to the right opportunities, I would teach people to open their hearts and minds. I asked to have any ego removed and to have their work be my focus. With a deep sigh of relief, I went back to the computer to check the ever-present flow of e-mails and found the very first one, from a total stranger.

Jill Lawrence wrote, "Mary Ellen, you do not know me, but would you like to be a guest on my radio show out of Seattle on Thursday?" Reading her e-mail, I laughed, thinking, "Be careful what you pray for. . . . It may arrive sooner than you think!" I also marveled at God's well-developed sense of humor. Jill said her Wisdom Radio show would be broadcast from the floor of the National Association of Broadcasters convention in Seattle. Not only would we be on the radio, but we would be live—for two hours and with an audience of professionals.

Talk about testing one's fears!

Jill's radio program was broadcast on October 26, 1998, ten months prior to the scheduled release date of August 2, 1999, for *Expect Miracles.* When I picked Jill up at the Seattle airport, a rainbow formed over her airplane as it taxied in to the terminal. Something magical was up, as if God was painting a picture for me.

I do not just write books about miracles. I *live* in the

world of Angels and miracles. Miracles surround us. Once we open our minds and hearts to them, they flood into our lives. For some of us, miracles are a way of life. Miracles hold the same power a prayer holds, the same energy your heart holds when you let God know you have the heartfelt intention to be a Divine Vehicle for miracles to flow through you to others. The wondrous result is that miracles will happen to you and through you.

Asking God for miracles is not about making a grocery list for God to fill. Rather, asking God for miracles is about asking to be of service, letting God know you are open and willing to be a vehicle for his/her energy to bring miracles into others' lives. It's that simple! In John F. Kennedy's famous speech, he said, "Ask not what your country can do for you. Ask what you can do for your country." Replace *country* with *God/Spirit,* and you will experience profound changes in your life.

A Christmas Filled with Miracles carries on the energy that was started by the Internet *Angels and Miracles Good-News-Letter* and continued in the book *Expect Miracles.* The stories in this book are all about Christmas and the miracles that happen at this powerful time of year. The book was created to share and invoke good news, miracles, and angelic inspiration among friends of all beliefs around the world. Enjoy this beautiful holiday book. It is sent from good and kind people who wish to share the magic of their miracles, and it is wrapped in love especially for you. Christmas can be all year long when we carry the spirit of the season in our hearts.

I begin this book by sharing a few of my own Christmas miracle stories. I wish you all joy and many miracles.

The Miracle of Love

I have a miracle story that I feel will allow others to heal, and it is with this intention of healing others that I share this very personal story.

My father left our family when my brother, sister, and I were pre-teens. Once gone, he did not want to continue a relationship with us. We were deeply hurt by his behavior, but life went on. My father had never said, "I love you" to any of us. Even as an adult, I ached to hear these words from him, but I knew hearing them was beyond a miracle; too much time had passed for him to say them.

A few weeks before Christmas 1998, I learned that cancer had invaded my father's body, and he had only six weeks to live. There was no hope for a cure. With great compassion for him, I sent a prayer request to our online prayer team, asking for strength and courage for him and his wife. Fifteen minutes after the prayer was sent by e-mail—or sent by my intentions to God's heart—the phone rang. It was my father. Dad rarely called me—maybe once a year—so I was startled to hear his voice, especially since I had just sent the e-mail for prayers for him.

Dad said, "What I have to say will be very difficult, but worth it, and I am going to try to make it through this call without crying." This man who could never show his emotions said, "I called to tell you I love you. I have always loved you. I have just never said it." He went on to say it was wrong that he had never said it and how he wished schools would teach children how to communicate with their families and teach parents how to talk to their children. Dad then bravely called my brother and sister and tearfully relayed his message of love to each of them. Once the ice is broken, it is easier to swim in the open waters.

My father spoke English and some Latin, German, and French. He was an executive for a powerful company in Canada. An electrical engineer, he was confident and in control of many situations and thousands of employees. Until this moment, however, this man had never said to his children, "I love you." As a young father, he had never bent down to hug and kiss his small children.

I share this story to inspire you and to offer you hope. I truly believe a miracle happened when my father phoned fifteen minutes after his name was put out to the prayer team. Please let this inspire you to call your family and let them know you love them. And if you have bridges to mend, consider mending them now. May that be the miracle this book holds for you.

The Barbie Doll

Growing up came early to my older brother, J.J., younger sister, Jo, and me. When the three of us were eight, ten, and twelve years old, our father left us. We had little money, and our mother had to get a job. After school we came home to a cold house, because my mother was not there and the furnace had been off all day. It seemed the warmth of the family was missing; it had gone out when our father left.

As Christmas approached, I knew we had no money for extras. I wanted a Barbie doll so much. My heart was broken with the realization that Christmas would never be the same as it had been before. Two weeks before Christmas, as I was cleaning the house, I put my mother's slippers away in her bedroom closet. I noticed a few hidden, carefully wrapped Christmas presents on the floor. One present looked to be the size and shape of a Barbie doll. I could not help myself as I peeked into the corner of the gift. Oh, how exciting—it was the much-wished-for doll! I carefully opened the gift wrapping and played with the doll for an hour each day for two weeks, until Christmas. After I had enjoyed the magic of the doll's long hair and pretty face, I would gently wrap her up so no one would notice. I could hardly wait to come home from school and unwrap her and escape into the magic of her being hidden away. At the time it was my only joy.

I will always remember that Christmas, not because of the beautiful doll, but because of the sacrifice I knew my loving mother had made to get the perfect gift for me. I learned from my mother that nurturing the spirit of a child is the greatest gift we can give.

Peanut Butter and Angels

One Christmas, to make a positive difference in others' lives, my daughter, Ariel, and I decided to deliver groceries to a local shelter for battered women. We have learned that it does not take much money or time to make a difference in someone's life.

Driving over to the bread outlet store, I was thinking that one of the hardest parts of being homeless must be being hungry all the time. I explained how oatmeal and dried soup mixes, nourishing foods that lasted a long time in the tummy, would be the wisest to buy. As I was reaching for the oatmeal, Ariel, who has "the gift," said, "Take them bread." I explained that oatmeal for breakfast would be better. Ariel said, "Mummy, the Angels are whispering to me. They say, 'Take bread.'" Who am I to argue with Angels? We bought a few bags of wholesome wheat and grain bread and drove over to the shelter.

When we walked into the shelter, there on the counter stood two of the biggest jars of peanut butter we had ever seen!

The person before us had just delivered the jars of peanut butter, and as you know, peanut butter goes better on bread than on oatmeal! We smiled at the Angels' guidance all the way home.

A Divine Long-Distance Phone Call

It was not going to be our usual Christmas. My mother's husband, Jim, had recently been diagnosed with terminal cancer, and, at the same time, my mother was in bed with an attack of gallstones. My husband and I would be spending Christmas with them, and we prepared for a Christmas visit that was going to be a difficult one.

My husband and I were not looking forward to leaving the comfort of our home on Vancouver Island, driving an hour to the ferry terminal, waiting in holiday traffic for the ferry, and then taking the lonesome one-and-a-half-hour trip over the gray waters to Vancouver, British Columbia. Before leaving Vancouver Island, I telephoned my best friend, Rita, and wished her a happy and a joyful holiday.

In the dark of the evening, the huge ferry boat finally docked in Vancouver. We drove through the torrential rain with our two Persian cats howling in the back seat of the car. We finally arrived at my mother's place, and I felt trepidation as I stepped into the house where I had spent so many Christmases. It was as gloomy inside the house as the weather was outside. No one was talking; my mother and Jim were both resting. The weight of their poor health was everywhere. It felt like the spirit of Christmas had been left behind on Vancouver Island with the joyful voices of our friends and neighbors.

We all went to bed early that Christmas Eve, almost

dreading the morning and thinking the spirit of the holiday season had evaporated with the diagnosis of Jim's cancer. I was the first one awake on Christmas morning. I knew Rita would be up, and I dialed her phone number. She picked up the telephone and said, "Hello," in a weak and crackling voice. I thought, *Oh no, what now! What else could possibly go wrong? Where was her sweet lyrical voice?* I asked if she was all right, and the voice on the other end said, "Who is this?" Apparently, I had awakened a total stranger on Christmas morning! I apologized and she said it was okay, as she had "no reason to get up and it was nice to talk to someone." My heart went out to this lonely woman and we started to chat. I learned that her name was Faith.

Rita's phone number was a long-distance call, so I was curious to know where Faith lived. She said she lived in Burnaby, a local calling number! To this day I cannot comprehend how this phone call had been rerouted to a total stranger like that. The phone numbers were not even similar! Faith was in her late seventies. Her husband had died seven years earlier. Her neighbor, a man in his twenties who always visited her, had left for the holiday to be with his fiancée. Faith had no reason to get up on Christmas morning, since she had no one to share Christmas with. Her Christmas Day was unfolding worse than ours; at least my family had each other.

Faith and I talked for an hour. We were laughing and sharing. I asked her to hold for a minute when I heard my mother stirring in her bedroom. I asked my mother if Faith could come and share Christmas dinner with us. She said, "Yes, Faith would be welcome." Faith was so excited. She'd had a long and lonely day looming ahead of her, and now she had something to look forward to. I told Faith how to come the fifteen miles on the bus. She had to hang up and call the bus station to see what the bus schedule would be for Christmas Day.

I hung up the phone, wondering what kind of woman was coming to dinner.

Faith later shared with us that while she was on the bus coming through town she was the only passenger. She wondered if she had made a good decision to leave the safety of her home and venture out to a total stranger's house. Faith told the bus driver of her "mystery morning phone call" that led her out on her adventure. She showed him our address, and he turned to her and said, "You will be fine in that neighborhood." But she was still uncertain and concerned.

Our formerly dreary home changed. My mother put on a dress and Jim mustered enough strength to put on a bright red shirt. I remember to this day how good he looked that last Christmas. The whole atmosphere of our home became one of joy.

We were awaiting the arrival of our mystery Christmas guest. Soon the aroma of the traditional Christmas turkey cooking wafted through the house. The time arrived for me to drive to the bottom of the hill and pick up our Christmas guest. There she was, slowly stepping off the bus. What a sweet face she had. Faith looked up at me, visibly relaxed. We smiled at each other, and she was the gift I took home to my family.

We had the nicest time, and a wonderful Christmas dinner. When it was late and time to drive Faith home to Burnaby, another miraculous event so unexplainable unfolded. As Faith was leaving, my mother realized they had not exchanged last names. We all were shocked when they did: they had exactly the same last name—

spelled the exact same way! Usually the last name was spelled with an "o," but theirs was spelled with an "e," a very rare spelling of the name. It was as if the phone call had linked us mysteriously to a relative. Faith had been married to a man from England, as Mum currently was. Faith's late husband and my mother's husband, Jim, were both the second children of four, and none of these siblings, once they married, had ever had a child. Both Faith's husband and Jim had the same combination of brothers and sisters in the same birth order. Faith and my mother had even gone to the same high school. So many "coincidences" came one right after the other. From the coincidences, we took faith knowing my mother would be fine and go on with her life after Jim's death, as Faith had after her husband's passing.

How was it possible to dial a long-distance number on Christmas morning and reach someone locally—someone who needed us, and whom we needed just as much? And how was it possible for both women to have married men with the same unusual family name? It was Divine intervention at its best!

Jim died a few months later. Faith has since passed on,

and every year before the holidays I phone my mother and we talk about the mysterious phone call, and we celebrate the marvel of our miracle Christmas guest. It still touches us deeply. The biggest gift to all of us that holiday was the realization that miracles do indeed happen.

My wish for you is a life filled with miracles!

Bless Your Angelic Heart,

Mary Ellen

Santa Is Coming to Town

I will never forget the Christmas in Vietnam when Santa Claus came to town.

It is always very, very hot in Vietnam in December. The temperature was over 100 humid degrees, and we were in the middle of the war. I was working at An Lac Orphanage, started by Mme. Vu Thi Ngai in Haiphong, and because of the response to the book *Deliver Us from Evil* written by Dr. Tom Dooley, we were able to give a home to thousands of children. After Dr. Tom's death in 1961, I took over the orphanage and sustained it until 1975 when I evacuated 219 babies.

The 121st Signal Battalion, 1st Infantry Division, which was stationed only ten miles away, had adopted our orphanage. The men decided to surprise the orphans and give them a Christmas party, so they wrote to their wives, sisters, and girlfriends back home and asked them to mail gifts for the children. Gifts wrapped in brightly colored holiday paper soon arrived at the base.

On Christmas Day, trucks piled high with hundreds of parcels arrived at our door. Just then we heard the whirl of a helicopter overhead and we all looked up. This sound generally meant our men were flying off into combat, so the sound was not a happy one for us. But this time the helicopter landed in a field across from the orphanage . . . and out came Santa Claus! Walking toward us in full regalia, complete with beard, in 100-degree humid heat, and with more gifts, came the first Santa any of the children had ever seen. A three-piece orchestra from the 121st Signal Battalion was playing "Silver Bells." The children joined in with "Jingle Bells"—a song I had taught them. They also sang "Auld Lang Syne" in Vietnamese. It was all so moving, and there wasn't a dry eye in the audience of soldiers.

We then tried to line up the children. There were almost 400 children lined up, rows and rows of them. And the soldiers of all ranks, all ages, sat side by side on the steps with the piles of gifts stacked up between them and handed them out to the children. As the children came up to receive their gifts they each put their hands across their chests and said, "Cam on," or, "Thank you" for the gift.

Major Bill Hilsman (now a general) and Sgt. Deeble and Lt. Fisher had conceived of the idea and put the festivities together. These were the true Angels of An Lac.

During the festivities, I looked up and saw a sight I will never forget. On the flat roof of the orphanage were our wonderful soldiers standing around the circumference, guns in readiness, protecting the children of An Lac and our staff of volunteers from possible snipers. At 4:00 P.M., the soldiers left us and returned to their base at Di-An; it was time to go back into the field of battle.

It truly was a Christmas I will always remember.

Author's Note: Twenty years later, in 1995, when I returned to find the orphans I had left behind, we had a reunion of sixty of the grown children; the first thing they did was sing "Jingle Bells."

Betty Tisdale

She Needed a
Miracle in Her Life

It was Christmastime, and I was chatting online with a woman I had never met. She was going through some really hard times: she was a single mother of three, quite ill, and unable to work. She had managed to get a Christmas tree, but she feared that except for the tree there would be no Christmas celebration. On top of that, her house desperately needed cleaning, and she was too ill to do it.

While talking to her online, I had an idea, but I didn't mention it to her. Later, also online, I contacted another friend who knows the woman personally and asked if he would be open to doing something for her and her children. He was all for it.

He and his wife went to the woman's home and cleaned the house and fixed a nice meal. My family and I took money we would have used to buy each other one gift and instead each bought a gift for this woman and her three children. We added to the package of gifts some bubble bath and scented lotion for her as well as some herbal teas and home-baked goodies. We sent this off to California by overnight express mail to reach the family in time for Christmas.

They were overjoyed! And, at the same time, we felt good to know we had turned an otherwise bleak and dreary time into a special Christmas for strangers. I would not have thought of helping this family without the help of my own Angel, who is always there if I just tune in. And I have found it takes so little to make a difference in the lives of others.

Myrna L. Smith

The Music Box

Twelve years ago, Stacey, our nineteen-year-old granddaughter, gave my husband and me the first Christmas present she had bought for us by herself. She was so excited she could not wait for us to open it, so she phoned long-distance and insisted we open the gift—right then, even though it wasn't yet Christmas.

Upon opening the cheerfully wrapped present, we discovered a beautiful music box. We decided to keep it in a special place on our bedroom bureau, with the simple switch on its electrical cord hidden behind the bureau. From time to time we would turn it on to listen to its wonderful music.

My husband died suddenly the following Valentine's Day. A few years later I carefully wrapped the music box along with my other belongings and moved from California to Washington. As I settled into my new home and unpacked the music box I placed it back in its cherished position on my bedroom bureau.

Last Christmas I was feeling especially melancholy at the loss of my husband; I thought of him all day long and wondered how he was doing in Heaven. That night I woke up to the sound of music. Our music box was playing . . . all by itself. It truly was the perfect Christmas present. My heart was at peace. I knew who had turned it on.

Frances S. Rossi

The Christmas Angel

Since he was three years old, our son Wade had participated in our church's annual Christmas pageant. Each year he received what he considered to be a "promotion." He started in preschool as a lamb and moved up each year—to a shepherd, a star, a resident of Bethlehem, and, finally, an Angel. As he was putting on his Angel costume, he commented to his Sunday school teacher, "I have waited all my life to be an Angel."

None of us realized how prophetic his statement was at the time. Soon afterward, at the age of ten, he lost his life in a horrific gas pipeline explosion as he was playing innocently with his friend.

During the Christmas season following the accident we received a card from his Sunday school teacher telling us of Wade's Angel comment, and adding, "I really believe Wade is an Angel since my Grandma always said the young ones become Angels right away."

We believe this to be true, and it is very comforting to us to know we now have our own special Angel.

Mary King

The Christmas Eve Gift

Twenty-eight years ago, when our daughter was a baby, my husband and I were having financial troubles. Times were really tough, and we knew Christmas was going to be lean this year—as it had been the year before.

We lived in a trailer in a mobile home park. When Christmas Eve came, along with it came some serious electrical problems. One of the outlets was spouting sparks and smoking. We had only $3 to our name. We knew we could not possibly afford an electrician, but neither could we ignore the situation.

We called a local fellow from the phone book, and he came right over. He worked on the problem for an hour and got it fixed. I held my breath. I hoped we might be able to pay him a little bit, week by week. I looked at him and asked, "How much do we owe you?" Maybe it was something in my voice, maybe it was something in my face. . . . I'll never know. He looked back at me, hesitated a minute, and then said, "You don't owe me anything. Merry Christmas."

Twenty-eight years is a long time, but I still remember this miraculous moment. Since then, I have tried, in one way or another, to repay him—by doing something for someone else. The spirit of Christmas was truly in this man. God bless him.

Aynne McAvoy

Santa's Helper

As I was going into a sporting goods store at Christmastime twenty years ago, I passed an obviously poor little fellow, about ten years old, playing imaginary basketball on the sidewalk. He was busy dribbling and shooting a nonexistent ball at a nonexistent basket. From time to time, he looked wistfully at a basketball in the window and then continued his imaginary game.

Several minutes later, while at the checkout counter, I looked out the store window. He was still playing. I told the clerk that I would buy a basketball and asked if he would pump it up to the correct pressure. I wrote a little note that read, "This ball is a gift from Santa Claus to _____," and I attached the note to the ball. I walked outside and then stopped to ask the little boy his name. I wrote his name in the blank space, and then said, "Billy, Santa asked me to give this to you and wish you a Merry Christmas!" I gave the bag containing the ball to Billy.

He had the most precious look of surprised joy and awestruck appreciation as he took the ball out of the bag and began to play! It was wonderful to see him playing ball with a real basketball.

I enjoyed doing this so much that every Christmas since, I look for a child who needs a toy, purchase one, and see to it a note from Santa is attached. Honestly, I think I do this more for me than for the child. Like so many others, I have always known the expression, "It is more blessed to give than to receive," and now I make a regular practice of giving to a child every Christmas. I truly feel what I receive from giving is very blessed indeed.

Robert E. Parrish, Ph.D.

Editor's Note: Dr. Bob died suddenly two weeks after he submitted this story. In his memory, many of us can literally pick up the ball and carry on his tradition.

Angels Love Hot Cocoa

A few days before Christmas, a bad ice storm hit our area. I am a trained professional driver, but I was scared to pieces driving home. I was concerned that another car might come skidding toward me on the ice. My hands gripped the wheel so tightly my knuckles were white.

I decided I needed a little help. I asked my Angels to ride on the hood of the car to keep me safe. Within moments, I felt them there. Soon, however, I decided it was not very nice for my Angels to be stuck on my car's hood in the middle of the freezing rain and sleet, so I "bundled them up" and "gave them some hot cocoa" while they rode on the hood. As scared as I was, it made me laugh out loud to think of my Angels on the hood, all bundled up under one blanket, drinking hot cocoa! As I saw this image, my fear eased up. Needless to say we all got home safely!

Recently a friend of mine told me that she "borrows" my Angels. Whenever the weather is bad, she asks my

Angels if they would come sit on her car. They arrive, she says, *with* their own blanket *and* hot cocoa! When they are on the hood, she feels them slowly turn around to look at her, letting her know they are warm.

I laughed and told her she could borrow my Angels whenever she wants, but her own Angels might feel bad! I explained, to her surprise, that she has Angels of her very own.

My wish for you this Christmas, for when you are out and about, is that you ride with your Angels. You won't be sorry!

Aynne McAvoy

The Star

I lost my beloved husband in 1995. On Christmas Eve of that year my boys and I went to the cemetery to visit his grave. While we were there I mentioned to the boys that I hoped he was with God.

In that instant I raised my eyes to the stars, and as we looked up we beheld a sight I have seen only in pictures: a star as bright as the one that shone the night Christ was born. It was shining brightly over the mountain behind the church where we were about to attend Christmas Eve service. It stayed there until we started into the church. Others who were walking toward the church commented on the sight as well.

The experience truly answered my question and left me filled with peace.

Myrna L. Smith

Miracles Beget Miracles

Two weeks before Christmas, I lifted something heavy at work and injured my back. I was in excruciating pain and could not walk or stand. After I got home, I was worried about not being able to work the following day and even wondered if I had injured myself badly enough so that I would not ever work again. The pain was so bad I feared I was going to have to go to the hospital.

Unable to do much else, I decided to rest in bed and watch TV. My ten-year-old granddaughter Jessica was with me. She said as we sat down together, "I love you so much Grandma. I am sorry you hurt."

Pax TV's show, *It's A Miracle,* was about to air; my friend Myrna Smith and her two sons were appearing on that night's episode. They had recently experienced a miracle, which Myrna had shared with me: The spirit of their late husband and father, Les, had gently visited all three of them at different times on Christmas Eve the year before.

Jessica and I settled in to watch the show. When the picture of Myrna's late husband, Les, was shown on the screen, I said to Jessica, "What a wonderful person Les was. He cared about people. He never complained of his hurts, and he always encouraged others with a smile, joke, or kind word. Les never said anything unkind about anyone."

At that moment the TV screen showed a reenactment of Les materializing in between Myrna and the Christmas tree. Suddenly I felt my injured leg begin to tingle. I also felt I was being told to stand, so I did. To my amazement there was no longer any pain in my back or leg. Jessica had the most astonished look on her face when I stood and moved around pain-free.

I am certain the love this man had for others was the catalyst; he was able to help me heal! I believe my faith allowed this miracle to happen.

Phyllis McLaughlin

Perfect Divine Timing

Estelle, a woman from Texas, became acquainted with our animal shelter in Canada when the shelter and its mission were featured in the Associated Press. Estelle began to correspond with Mother Cecilia Mary, our Mother Superior, after reading the story. (The shelter has since closed.)

Estelle wrote to us once a week over a period of twenty years. During this time, she did not share much about herself except that she had cats. When Mother Superior, because of her age and failing health, could no longer personally write back to Estelle, I took Mother's place and answered Estelle's letters.

One winter Estelle wrote and mentioned she was feeling very cold when she came home from work in the evenings. I had a sense Estelle was not well off and asked a few of my friends to send her presents for Christmas. I did not know what size she was, but people sent clothing, sweaters, jackets, and gloves. One woman sent a large pair of boots.

Estelle wrote us back and said, "I never told you my size, age, or where I live. I must tell you I am a tiny little woman." We had a laugh reading her letter—the boots we had sent were huge! Estelle went on to write that she lived in a small shack with her cats in the countryside in Texas. She was alone after having cared for her aging parents.

Toward the spring she wrote a tearful letter to say that she had gone to work that morning and when she arrived, her fellow workmates in the clothing factory all sang "Happy Birthday" to her. It was the first time in her life anyone had ever celebrated her birthday. Then her boss handed her a pink slip because she had turned eighty years old that day, and she had to retire. Estelle spent the spring and summer on the farm cleaning it up to the best of her ability and enjoying her life with her cats. She never said much about her living conditions or herself in the letters, which continued to arrive every week.

Late in the fall the letters stopped. I didn't know why and we had no contact in her area to find out. After a month, the absence of her letters became a terrible concern for me. One night, close to Christmas, I tossed and turned and thought about it all night. In the morning, I called my friend Gail in Bellevue, Washington, and said, "You are associated with a newspaper. Do you have a newspaper contact who works in Estelle's town? Would you please call them and ask them to try and find out something about Estelle?"

Two hours later Gail called me back in Canada and said they had found Estelle. The sheriff had gone out to check on Estelle after the local newspaper called him. He found her covered with new-fallen snow, with her cats on top of her keeping her warm. Apparently Estelle had fallen and could not get up. Then it had started to snow, and the snow began to blanket her. At the hospital, the doctors said another few minutes out in the snow and she would have been dead. There had been an absence of letters for more than a month, so it is a mystery why I had such a strong urge to contact her the same day she needed help desperately.

While Estelle regained her strength in the hospital, another miracle unfolded. Estelle did live in a little shack on the outskirts of town. She was very old and frail, and had no electricity, no running water, and only an old wood stove. I wrote a letter about Estelle to my friend Frank in California. I wasn't asking him for anything; I was just so heartbroken I wanted to write about her. In no time at all, however, I received a letter back from Frank. After reading my letter, he took the initiative, contacted the town's sheriff, and asked the sheriff to make sure Estelle had water, electricity, a proper fireplace for heat, and a color TV. These wonderful gifts all came to fill her home during the magic of the Christmas season. When Estelle arrived home from the hospital, her joy at the change in her little shack was enormous. She was overwhelmed with appreciation.

Frank is in no way a wealthy man. He could not easily afford to make the world brighter for Estelle, and yet he sacrificed to make life better for her. His generosity reminded me of how my mother treated people, with love for strangers. It was heartwarming to see the practice continuing on.

Sister Mary Julia, O.S.B.

A Miraculous
Christmas Reunion

This is a continuation of the story I told in the book *Expect Miracles*. In that story, I shared the experience of one of my student's mothers, Susan Roy. Susan is a home health care nurse. The week before Christmas, by Divine guidance, Susan arrived at 444 Elm Street, Apartment 111, to care for a newly assigned patient, Miss Brown. In fact, Susan had been scheduled by her office to be at 444 Maple Street, Apartment 111, to care for a different Miss Brown! The Miss Brown at the mistaken address was in need of home health care too; Susan cared for this Miss Brown, because she thought she had been assigned to her case. Hours later, she learned of her mistake, at which time she felt certain Divine intervention had brought her to the mistaken address to care for this woman who was so in need of help. It was truly remarkable that not only were the addresses almost identical, and only one street apart, but also both ladies had the same last name, and both were in need of home health care.

The continuation of this wonderful story is as follows: Shortly after Christmas, Susan was told how her "mistake" had become another miracle. She had left a business card at the home of the Miss Brown she had cared for. Because of Susan's excellent care, Miss Margaret Brown called to request home health care service and Susan's help. As the people on the staff at the office were filling out the forms for the new client, they began to notice many similarities between Miss Margaret Brown's information and what was on file for Miss Audrey Brown, who was already receiving regular care. The office compared their personal information and realized the two women were sisters, and then discovered, to everyone's complete surprise, the ladies had not seen each other in more than thirty years!

Susan, in her off-duty hours, arranged a time for the sisters to get together for tea, and introduced them to each other. Susan told me, "Lots of hugs, tears, and stories followed as the sisters had been thinking and wondering about each other for years."

Their miracle meeting evolved over the Christmas holidays. Susan turned out to be not only a home health care worker for the two sisters but their miracle worker too. "It was absolutely wonderful to watch," Susan said. "I left the two sisters together and felt it was beyond a miracle. After thirty years, they got to be reunited with each other, and for that I am so grateful."

Susan truly offers Divine service. I wonder who her boss really is?

Kathe Kenny

Christmas Angel

On Christmas Eve, my friends and I helped to prepare dinner that would be served on Christmas Day at a local shelter. We returned to the shelter on Christmas Day to sing carols while the shelter's men, women, and a handful of children enjoyed their Christmas dinners.

Later, the excited children, from toddlers to young teens, clamored for a place in line to receive toys from Santa Claus. There was a small girl among them, looking lost, bewildered, and alone in the crowd. She was about my grandson's age, three years old; she was neatly dressed and her hair was beautifully braided. I picked her up and held her in my arms. I noticed her eyes were blank. There was no light in them, no joy, no excitement, not even any recognition of what was happening around her. I found a baby doll for her. To my surprise, she did not reach for the doll or respond to it any way. I held her close, rocked her, and quietly sang to her; I wondered what this child had experienced to make her eyes so vacant, so unresponsive, so joyless. Eventually, and very reluctantly, she reached for the doll and lovingly held onto it. She wrapped her other arm tightly around my neck and rested her little head on my shoulder as I continued to gently rock her and sing to her. She sank into my arms, relaxed, and seemed content to be held and to rest. A sense of peacefulness came over me.

We stood there for some time until the children began to leave. When I found her family, I placed her in her mother's arms. I learned she was one of eight children—and her name was Angel. Miraculously, on this Christmas Day, Spirit/God/All That Is had placed an Angel in my arms to guide me into my heart, to help me understand more about myself, and to me teach how very blessed I really am.

Linda Adler

The Most Decorated House

It was almost Christmas, and I wanted to hand-deliver a Christmas card to a friend to let her know how much I appreciated her friendship. I drove to her neighborhood but soon got lost. I was driving at night, I couldn't recognize where I was, and I had neglected to bring her address with me. After many turns and streets that didn't look familiar, I decided to stop at a house and ask for a telephone book and call her for directions. I am hearing impaired so this is not as easy for me as it might be for the average person.

I asked out loud for my Angels' help in finding my friend's house. "Please let the help come from the house with the most Christmas decorations and lights in the neighborhood. And, let the person I ask be someone who would be more than willing to help me locate my friend's home."

I drove slowly and traveled down another few streets. My eyes fell on a brightly lit home. It had colorful lights and beautiful decorations all over the house, trees, yard, fence—everywhere! In awe, I turned into the driveway and heard joyful music coming from inside. When two children answered the door, I asked for their mother. The mother arrived with a big smile and said, "Yes?" I explained my situation and requested her phone book. She happily went to get it. I found my friend's number, and the woman handed me her telephone.

The phone's volume was too low for me to hear. I explained to the woman I couldn't hear the phone because of my deafness. She said it was her pleasure to make the call for me. As she was dialing my friend's phone number, she asked me for the first name of the person she should ask for. I said Joy. The lady's eyes widened, and she exclaimed, "Joy! I know Joy!" The woman then said, "Follow me and I will lead you to her home." I was so thankful for her kindness and help!

I had asked the Angels to send me to a friendly, decorated home. The woman they directed me to not only helped me but also knew my friend Joy, and then led me to Joy's house. Miracles do happen when you ask.

Jeanne Kvarda

There is Room Enough in Santa's Sleigh

I am a single mother of three children. My son Dillon had wanted a toy "ride-on" motorcycle for about six months, and he asked for one as his Christmas wish. The battery-operated toy motorcycle weighs ninety pounds, travels five miles per hour, and costs $350. Instead of breaking his spirit and telling him, "No, I don't have the money for a ride-on motorcycle," I told him to pray for a motorcycle and God would make it happen. I thought that I was keeping his spirit alive and he would eventually forget the motorcycle and move on to a cheaper wish for Christmas.

Well, he didn't forget, and he didn't move on to a cheaper wish, either. So, when we went to visit Santa Claus, he asked him for a ride-on motorcycle. In a quiet voice, Santa assured him, "There is room enough in the sleigh this year for a ride-on motorcycle." My face dropped in disbelief. I didn't have the money for this

Christmas wish. I didn't know how I was going to break it to Dillon that, in fact, he wouldn't be getting a motorcycle this year.

I sat Dillon down and started to explain to him that Santa would not be able to deliver on his promise. I hadn't gotten out more than two words when Dillon looked deeply into my eyes with great conviction and said, "Mom, don't you remember, 'There is room enough in Santa's sleigh' for my motorcycle?" I didn't know what more to say, because I couldn't bring myself to break his heart. I dropped the subject. He was certain that what Santa had told him was true.

The next day I went to work. While sitting in my office the very clear thought came to me that I should ask my sales director to help me find this motorcycle for my son. With the help of my sales director and his contacts I was able to find an incredible, top-of-the-line, ride-on motorcycle for Dillon at a price I could easily afford while still making the Christmas wishes of his siblings come true, too.

None of this could have occurred without the help of God, Angels, and the strong conviction of a six-year-old boy. My son taught me that miracles happen, especially if we believe they can. Because my son knew there was "room enough in Santa's sleigh" that year for a ride-on motorcycle, one appeared. And God knew that I, his mother, wanted to nurture his spirit, so with the help of Earth Angels, a miracle happened for my family at Christmas.

Lilas (Hanebuth) Asher

Special Delivery

We live in Live Oak, a very small community in California. When my granddaughter Jessica was eight, she was cold all the time because of a medication she had to take. She would always wear layers of clothes and wrap herself in blankets.

Everyone in her family loved to play in the snow. Jessica did, too, but her hands would get very cold, and her mittens were not the greatest. For Christmas, she decided to write Santa and ask him for new mittens that would keep her hands warm. She told him how much she would like to stay out in the snow and throw snowballs and build snowmen and play as long as the others did. Her sister and brother and cousins wrote letters, too. The other children all wanted big and costly presents. Her mother asked her to put something else in her note to Santa. Jessica said, "No, mom, having fun in the snow is the thing I want most." The letters were mailed early in December.

Christmas Eve morning a package arrived in the mail

for Jesse from Santa Claus. When she opened it, she was overjoyed with a beautiful, warm pair of ski gloves in just her size. Her joy was immeasurable, and the rest of us delighted in her excitement. While watching it I felt housed right in very Heart of God. Tears poured down my face in gratitude and love. To this day, we have no idea where the gloves came from and who the wonderful Santa Claus was. We tried to get information from the post office, but there was no record of the gift having been sent or received—nothing! But the sweetness of it and the simplicity of how much happiness can come from something so small will always make this my favorite Christmas.

Love comes in small packages, and what is given with love, no matter how small, is the greatest gift of all.

Marie Rhodes

There Is a Santa

In the 1980s, I was a single mom with two daughters. I was living with money anxieties and fears about my competence as a parent and the usual single mother guilt. I was constantly balancing work and home, forever struggling with money worries. One day we came home to find the electricity and water had been turned off; I hadn't been able to pay those bills.

Christmas was approaching, and once again it found me unprepared and with no money. My paycheck wasn't going to stretch far enough to include presents and decorations and holiday food. We went to a friend's farm and cut down the loneliest tree for our living room. The tree was a bit sparse, and we used duct tape to attach a branch to fill it in a little. To brighten up the poor tree we tied hair bows and scarves on it.

The days passed and I had no idea of what to do for Christmas. Then, there were only two shopping days left, and I was a wreck. I started to panic as I realized there would not be any presents from Santa.

Did I pray? I don't remember specifically, but I do know that when life was really bleak, I would cry for help and talk to my Angels. So, I talked to my Angels and asked for help. When I got up to get dressed for work the next day, I opened the top dresser drawer to get a bracelet. I always keep my jewelry in the top drawer on a brown towel liner. The liner was rumpled that morning, and when I picked it up to straighten it, underneath I found a $100 bill!

The girls woke up to my sobbing. I was sitting on the edge of my bed, money in hand, weeping. "I found this," I said, "in my drawer." "There is a Santa Claus," I told them. "Today, Santa is my Guardian Angel." There is no other possible explanation for the money showing up in the drawer except that I was the recipient of a Christmas miracle. I shopped for gifts and food. My girls had presents Christmas morning under the tree

I thank my Angels for sticking with me through the times I wasn't listening, wasn't willing to learn, or was being stubborn. I have always said mine are the Angels in tattered robes, and I am grateful for their dedication to and perseverance with me.

May the love of God's gifts find you today and every day.

Susan Caldwell

Miracles Afoot

On New Year's several years ago, about 1:00 A.M., my soon-to-be husband, Roger, decided to visit a friend on the other side of our subdivision. He opted to ride his son's bike on this moonlit night. It had snowed earlier, and there was a light dusting on the frozen ground.

Going too fast on the bike, he whipped around a bend in the road and fell off the bike. My husband is nearsighted and as blind as a bat. His head and face hit the concrete when he fell, knocking off his glasses. He crawled around, searching all over the road trying to find them when he came across a huge pair of tennis shoes . . . with feet in them. Roger was amazed to find someone outside at 1:00 in the morning. He looked up to find a teenager staring down at him.

The teen said, "Is there something wrong, Mister?" Roger told him he had lost his glasses and couldn't find them. The teen quickly located them, unbroken, about fifteen feet away and gave them to Roger. Then the young man asked Roger if he needed anything else. Roger said, "Yeah, some coffee!" They went into the young man's house, where no one was home, and began to talk. Roger is an incessant and wonderful talker who always says the right things and makes everyone feel good, and he loves kids. He is like a Pied Piper around young people.

The teen was visiting from New England and, as they talked, Roger realized the young man was suffering from a terrible depression. The boy had been outside at that hour because he was on his way to the river to commit suicide. Roger was there to talk him out of it. He was able to give the young man positive talk and new hope, and the teen said things like, "I'd never looked at things that way before." He thanked Roger with all of his heart and soul when they parted.

Why did Roger venture out on that road that night, at that precise time, and fall practically at the young man's feet? Roger felt good when he realized he was there to save the teen and convince him there is faith, there is love, and there is someone above and beyond us. They both acknowledge this miracle.

A "coincidence"? They believe it was an act from God.

Dale S. Westerberg

Christmas Eve Dinner

The Christmas of 1980 I was twenty-one years old and in the final year of my four-year enlistment in the U.S. Air Force.

I was stationed at Griffiss Air Force Base near the small town of Rome in upstate New York. It was a typically cold, upstate New York kind of day—gray and overcast with a blustery cold wind. I had just finished working my shift and was excited about heading home for Christmas leave. I didn't have enough leave to take off the entire week before Christmas, so I was working right up through Christmas Eve. I disliked having to head home at the last moment, but I wanted to save the little bit of leave time I had for the week after Christmas, so I could be home for New Year's Day, too. I knew the drive well; I had made the trip home to Maryland from upstate New York several times during the previous year and a half. I was looking at a seven-hour drive if all went smoothly. As with past trips, my car was already packed so I could simply jump in and head for the highway.

December days in upstate New York are very short, and the sun was already setting when I pulled onto the highway. I felt a little less confident of a trouble-free drive this time as my trusty old Chevy was now eleven years old and had more than 160,000 very hard miles on it. The New York winters had been rough on it, and it was showing its age. Still, at that moment it was purring like a kitten, so off into the night I went, south to Binghamton and then to the New York-Pennsylvania border—no problems.

Then I noticed the first few snowflakes.

Getting weather reports for other states was not easy back then, and as usual, I had not taken the time to get the forecast before hitting the road. It would not have mattered; I was less intimidated by things back then, and I wanted to be home for Christmas so badly that I would have driven even if a blizzard had been forecast. By the time I entered the Pennsylvania Turnpike, the snow had become much heavier and wetter. Traffic was moving at less than forty miles per hour.

I began listening to weather reports and, sure enough, a full-blown winter storm was just beginning.

It was now 8:00 P.M. I had been on the road for four hours and, because of the traffic, I knew there were another four hours ahead of me. I was beginning to feel the first twinge of panic, worrying about getting stuck—I was not dressed for winter survival. I was out in the middle of nowhere with no heavy clothing and a car that overheated if it idled for very long. I feared I would freeze to death if I had to pull over.

The storm had now become a virtual whiteout, and the weather reports were predicting several more hours at this intensity with many inches of accumulation expected. The temperature had plummeted to just below the freezing mark and the snow was beginning to clump up on my windshield wipers. This was causing the wiper to lift from the surface and slide uselessly over the rapidly accumulating slush.

My defrosters were now wide open, and yet I could clear less than half of my windshield. I didn't dare to pull over as the slush and snow had reached danger-ously high accumulations at the road shoulders and had already begun to claim victims. In desperation, I low-ered the window and tried to clear the wiper by slapping it as it went by. This quickly became futile; the wet snow had become rock-hard ice. There was now only a small circle of clear windshield, and this was getting smaller with each pass of the wiper. The turnpike had now become absolutely treacherous.

Finally, I arrived at my exit and soon was in an area called Brandywine. I knew that road construction was going on in the area. In the middle of a snowstorm, nothing seems familiar anyway, so all I could do was hope that in all this crazy weather I was somehow still on the right path to home. With all the excitement, I had not been watching my gauges. I knew that soon after getting off of the turnpike I would need to fill up the tank.

During previous trips I had always been able to reach Brandywine with a quarter tank to spare. But this time because of the traffic and weather I had used much more gas, and the fuel gauge needle was on the wrong side of "E." With all of the construction and detours, it would have been difficult to find a gas station in good weather; in a snowstorm this simple task had become all but impossible. As ominous as the gas gauge was, it was the temperature gauge that had my attention now.

The temperature gauge was nearing the boiling-over

mark. I really became scared. I had only a vague idea of where I was, I couldn't see any signs of civilization for what appeared to be miles, and I now knew for certain the car's forward progress was about to end. Just then, an eighteen-wheeler rushed past and threw a wave of frozen slush up over my windshield and covered the remaining area of clear glass. Within the next second I knew I was in for a rough landing. I allowed the car to drift off to the right side of the road and into what appeared to be a very small parking lot. As I pulled into the lot, I noticed a small motel.

The car came to a stop, and with the engine spitting and sputtering I turned it off. Suddenly I was immersed in an eerie silence broken only by the howling of the wind outside. I suspected the storm had interrupted electrical power in the community, because I didn't see any lights on in any of the individual motel units, and I couldn't tell which unit was the office. It wouldn't have mattered anyway as I didn't have my checkbook with me nor did I have much cash. I also didn't have credit cards. I felt like the poster child for poor planning.

Fortunately, there was a pay phone right outside the motel, and I placed a collect call to my parents. Thank

God the phone was functioning. I told them how much trouble I was in and asked if my brother could use his four-wheeler to come and get me. Within minutes they were underway. But they were at best four hours away. Not sure they would be able to find me, I got back into my car to wait and began to pray.

What I hadn't realized was that the owners of the motel were observing me from their window. The proprietors were a young couple with two young children. They had been enjoying a quiet and snowy Christmas Eve when they saw me dressed in my military uniform wandering around their parking lot and shivering in the phone booth. They invited me into their home, which was part of the motel office, and made me feel right at home. They fed me dinner and holiday cake. What an amazing turn of events! Just moments before, I had been freezing and scared and now I was warm, sitting in front of their fireplace with a blanket over my shoulders and a hot meal in my stomach.

I remember how incredibly welcome these wonderful people made me feel. How dangerous it must have seemed to take a complete stranger into their home, especially when they had two young children. Of all the places I could have broken down, what a turn of good fortune it was to be forced off of the road at that location, and what a blessing it was to meet these people. I had prayed, and I have no doubt someone up there was watching over me.

My brother and father arrived at midnight. They expected to find me near-frozen and were surprised when they walked into the den and saw me sipping sherry in front of the warm fire. They just shook their heads and smiled. We all knew what a blessing it was, and nothing more needed to be said. We thanked the young couple and headed home. It wasn't until some time later I realized I had forgotten to get their names, something I still regret. I have thought about the experience, the couple's kindness, and the miracle many times through the years. If you are reading this story now . . . thank you and Merry Christmas.

Charles (Skip) F. Englehart

A Hug for Santa

I remember Christmas as a child of poor parents. I hesitated to ask for gifts because I knew how tight money was at home. Because of their poor health and lack of education, my parents struggled to make ends meet. Asking for gifts would put an additional financial strain on them, and the thought of my father having to take an extra job to pay for the toys—which is what he would do—was more than I could bear. And so when they'd ask, "Patrick, what is your Christmas wish for Santa this year?" I'd say, "Nothing. I'd just be happy to hug him."

And what a shock it was to the Santa at the Sears store, when, after I'd been waiting in the long line for hours, I'd hop up on his lap and he'd say, "Ho ho ho, now there, what would you like for Christmas, young man?" and I'd answer, "Nothing Santa, I just wanted to see you and hug you." This was always met with complete surprise and disbelief. Santa would turn to the other children waiting in the line and say, "Nothing? Do you hear that kids, this young man doesn't want anything for Christmas."

But it was true. I'd grown so used to not wanting anything material, I truly did not care what I received or if I received anything at all. What I most wanted was to have my family together and to hug Santa. On Christmas Eve, I'd go outside and look up into the cold night sky, watching the stars, hoping to see Santa in his sleigh and wishing with all my heart that he would come to my house and spend the whole night playing with me under the tree. This was my idea of a great Christmas: having my family together and hugging Santa.

Patrick J. Murphy

The Children of the World

On one of my trips to Egypt, something miraculous happened.

One morning as I walked to the *souk* (a street where vendors sell things in small shops), I saw a little street child. She was only four or five years old. This tiny child was picking up old, dirty, half-eaten bread from the city street and eating it. She was not asking people for money; she was foraging for food. When I saw this, I knew I had to do something.

I went over and in my best half-Arabic and half-English, I tried to speak with her. The dirty little street child looked up with beautiful brown eyes. She stepped back, frightened. I took her small hand in mine and walked along the shops asking in Arabic, "Do you speak English?" until I found a man who said, "Yes, why?" I then asked him to tell the little girl to follow me to the nearest food cart and I would buy her food. He asked, "Why would you do such a thing for a beggar?" I told him, "She has not begged me for anything, she was eating off the street!" He told the little girl what I had said. Then I asked him, "How much should it cost me for the pocket bread with beans in it?" He smiled and told me 2 pounds, or about 50 cents. He walked with us to the food cart; once there he told the man at the cart what I was doing and helped me to buy three pocket breads. I gave one to the little girl, and she ate it as if she had not eaten for days. The other two I put into a bag and handed to her. She smiled a wondrous smile and ran off.

The next morning on my way to the *souk,* the little one was waiting. She obviously knew a good thing when she saw it. I laughed and said, "Okay, breakfast again?" and repeated the ritual of the day before, thinking that for at least fourteen days, the length of my stay in Cairo, this little one would have breakfast and maybe lunch, depending on whether or not she was sharing the other pocket breads with others. The shopkeeper smiled and so did the cart vendor. We seemed to have become fast friends over this little deed.

That night I got to thinking about my little street urchin. She was so dirty and smelled so badly. What else could I do to help her? The next morning I was off to the *souk* again but this time I had a bigger plan. As I came around the corner, right on time, there she was, waiting and smiling. I took her hand and went over to the shop-keeper and asked, "Where is there water?" He thought I wanted bottled water to drink and I explained, "No, I want a faucet, like where the people wash before prayers." He looked at me like "Now you really are a crazy American!" and then he showed me a little side alley where there was a water faucet. "Okay, here goes," I thought. "What will these people think? But, oh well." I reached into my bag and pulled out a newspaper and laid out a soap bar, a washcloth, shampoo, and cream rinse (the kind you get in nice little bottles at good hotels). Now for the hard part: getting her out of her rags without upsetting everyone.

The water was cold, but it was the best I could do. Off came her clothes and I started soaping her down. She wiggled and squirmed the whole time and I could tell by the smile on her face how she loved having someone care for her. It took two soapings to clean her and all the shampoo to help her smell wonderful. Out of my bag I pulled a towel and dried her off. Then I pulled out a little dress from the bag I was carrying. I had purchased the dress for a friend's child who, I decided, could do with one less dress this year. This little one needed it more. As I lifted the dress out, and she saw it, her face lit up like any child's at Christmas. The dress was a little big, but she would grow into it.

Then I noticed something: a crowd had gathered. I had been so intent on my cleanup job I had not noticed them. I looked up into the beaming faces of men, women, and other children. The shopkeeper asked why I was helping this child, and my answer was, "The children of the world are mine and yours. If we don't care for them, who will?" I told him this child was as much mine as if I had given birth to her, that we are all responsible for the children, and if one child went to bed hungry, then we were not doing our part. He turned to the crowd and translated to them and they began to nod their heads "Yes" in agreement. To my surprise they all began to loudly applaud. It was as if in this single little act of helping this child, a miracle had happened. I bent and wrapped the old dress and the soap and things into a plastic bag and gave it to the girl before we went off to get her morning breakfast. Things had changed: the food vendor would not take money and gave her food himself. She and I hugged, and I went off to do my work.

The next day, I had many business matters to attend to and didn't go to the *souk*. Then I became ill and was not able to go for five days. On the sixth day I walked the street looking for her, and there she was, in her new dress. The shopkeeper came running up and said, "Madame, I thought you must have gone home." I said no, I had been ill, and he told me not to worry, they had made sure she had food each day. "But," he said, "each morning she would set out looking for you for hours. I tried telling her you had gone back to America and she would say no, and wait."

I asked the man whether, if I gave him $40, which would cover about a year of food, he would make sure she was fed each day. He said, "Yes" and that others would help too, as they felt Allah had sent me as a teacher to them. I laughed and thought, Spirit at work again. The day before I left Cairo, I sat down with the little girl and the shopkeeper as our translator, and had him tell her I was leaving. I told her she would be fed each day, and I would try to come back next year. I brought her a bag of fruit bars, soap, shampoo, some money, and a sweater much too big, but it would still keep her warm.

Where her parents are, I do not know. But this I do know—one person can make a difference to a child. If on each trip I am able to touch a child, then I have done Spirit's work. The children of the world are truly mine and yours.

Atira Hatton

The Christmas Sock

My father, Sidney McMaster (born 1893), came from a family of seven children. He was the third youngest. His father left when the children were young and, as a result, my father had to leave school at the age of nine so he could go to work to help support his mother and two younger siblings. His older siblings had done the same before they had grown up and moved out of the home. My father got a job as an office messenger, and he also sold programs at the circus part-time. One day, he met the headmaster of the local school, who offered to give him tuition so he could take classes. He was able to take courses at night until he completed his schooling.

Johannesburg, South Africa, was a mining town when he was growing up. On Christmas Eve, the town would become alive with the spirit of Christmas. People were rushing about, shopping for their Christmas dinner and last minute gifts. But times were tough for my father and his family. He was upset because there would be no celebrations in their home—there just wasn't enough money to make it festive.

While walking down the main street amidst the hustle and bustle, he saw a sock tied up in a knot, lying in the gutter beside the sidewalk. Something prompted him to move it with his foot, and when he felt something heavy inside, he bent down to pick it up. To his astonishment and delight, it was filled with coins! He was amazed! In the midst of all the people bustling about, he had found this treasure. The sock full of coins was an answer to his prayers, and he hurried to the nearest food store and bought a turkey and a few other items for a celebration. He also bought a small gift each for his mother and younger sister and brother.

Because of this Christmas miracle my father's faith in God became very strong. The miracle made him determined to improve his career and to continue his studies at night. He got a degree in Accountancy and Company Secretarial and eventually became secretary to Sir Abe Bailey, a well-known mining magnate. He continued to pursue his studies and became estates manager of one of the biggest mining houses in South Africa, the Anglo-

American Corporation. By the time of his retirement, after forty-five years of service, and with his determination and strong religious principals, he had been able to send our family of six children to private Catholic schools, the best private schools in South Africa. He always had great compassion for the poor and was a member of the Society of St. Vincent de Paul, visiting the poor and the sick and collecting and distributing food parcels and clothing for more than forty years.

Every Christmas he never failed to tell us the story of the sock and of his Christmas Miracle! My strong belief in miracles and Angels came from him. I grew up knowing that my Angels, especially my Guardian Angel, were always beside me.

Anne Bayley

The Snow Angels

When I was in Montana four years ago, visiting my daughter and her family, we all went out into the woods and cut down our Christmas tree. It was new experience for me, as I live in Southern California by the beach. It had snowed the night before—the most beautiful, white, soft, powdery, diamond-sparkling snow you ever saw. I had never made a snow Angel before, so I flopped into the soft snow, laughing hard with my daughter, Robin, and two granddaughters, Jennifer and Lacy, and moved my arms and legs to make a snow Angel. Robin, Jennifer, and Lacy did the same. We were all lined up in a straight row in the snow, making our Angels.

The sun was out, the sky was intensely blue, and fluffy white clouds drifted overhead. And, you can guess what we saw in the sky above us as we looked skyward. . . . I asked my granddaughters what they saw, and without hesitating they answered, "Four Angels, Nana!" And they were right. Drifting very slowly over our heads were four perfectly formed huge cloud Angels, all in a line, which I had no doubt represented the four of us lying on our backs, in a form of our own Heaven on Earth.

What an unforgettable moment to see four heavenly cloud Angels looking down at the four of us looking up at them, marveling at the sight of such unexpected beauty. There was no wind in the sky, and the cloud Angels stayed with us for several minutes, their images indelibly imprinted on my heart forever.

Katie Cole

The Birthday Twins, the Marines, and Christmas

In 1988, several of my Marines buddies and I were returning home for the Christmas holidays from Augusta, Georgia, where we had just finished a week of training. We stopped in a small town at a McDonald's restaurant on our way back to Charleston. As we pulled up to the pay window, the clerk was taking an order from a woman in the car behind us; she had requested two Happy Meals. We heard a small voice over the speaker yell, "Mommy, it's our birthday and we want cheeseburgers!" The mother's voice, tingling with embarrassment, said, "No, all we can afford are hamburgers." The clerk then said "Happy Birthday" to the children and asked if the woman wanted anything else. She replied, "No, we are on our way to Charleston for Christmas to visit the children's grandparents, and we can only afford the two Happy Meals for the twins' fifth birthday."

As the clerk at the pay window turned to me to take our money, I asked how much the woman owed for her meals. She told us the total; we paid it, and gave her an extra $5 so the woman could purchase a meal for herself. The four of us then each put 10 bucks in a pot, and asked the clerk to give it to the woman and tell her the money was for her to purchase something for her and her kids in Charleston the next day. The clerk asked if we knew her, and we replied, "No, it doesn't make a difference. If she asks who it came from, just say the Charleston Marines."

We continued on our way, and stopped for gas an hour later. A car pulled up behind us, and a woman and two children got out and came over to us. They asked if we were the Charleston Marines who had purchased meals for them. We were all a little embarrassed, but we admitted we were. She thanked us, gave each of us a hug, and asked for our names. We declined. Who we were was not important. When we were getting ready to return to our cars, the young boy walked up to one of the guys, grabbed his trousers, and said, "One day I want to be a Marine." This brought laughter to us all (and later it brought tears as we thought of what he had said).

If anyone had seen all of us standing there, they would have thought we had known one another for years. Some of us had been stationed together only for a few weeks, and we certainly didn't know the woman and the children, but in the end, we were all members of God's family. This may not seem like a miracle to you, but pretend you are five and you want cheese burgers for your birthday. . . and they suddenly appear. Miracles come to all of us at any age and kindness seems to be the magical ingredient that heralds them in.

Eddie de Roulet

A Holiday Angel

Over the holidays, my son used his boat to go to his friend's home. He was on his way back home when he called from a local dock to say his boat had run out of gas. He had used his hands to paddle in to the dock. I threw a can of fuel into the car and drove over to help him. On my way, I praised God and the Angels for keeping him safe.

When I arrived at the dock I found out my son hadn't tied the boat well and had had to swim after it in the icy Northwest waters. I got him into my warm coat and gave him the gas for the boat. I then returned to my car and watched to make sure he left safely for home. As I watched, a man emerged from an opening in a nearby fence. He walked around my car without meeting my gaze or looking at the beach. The man was older than me and had the most beautiful golden blonde hair—enviable, I thought! I watched as my son backed his boat away from the beach. I saw the man walk purposefully toward and onto the dock. I wondered if this was his morning walking routine.

Twenty minutes after I returned home, my son rushed into the house. "Hurry Mom. Get me back to the dock. I've left my duffel bag with my new shoes and sunglasses and all my other stuff there!" Precious stuff he couldn't afford to replace—and things that should not have gone for any boat ride. He was beside himself, frozen and practically in tears. Sending my Angels on ahead, I grabbed the keys and we sped toward the dock. I said, "Just pray, Honey," silently praying we would find the duffel, and thanking God that my husband had finally gotten my car fixed the previous evening!

The kid was inconsolable. "Hang onto your faith, Honey, that's what you've got it for. God will not let you down, He never does. He knows how important this is to you, and it's just as important to Him." I thanked Him and the Angels in advance for taking care of this for us! We made it to the dock in two minutes, and could immediately see that his bag was gone. We were both so disappointed. I mentioned the man I had seen, and I said I'd find him and see if he had secured the bag for us. I followed the path the man had come from. I then entered through the opening in the fence and onto the deck of a beach house. A woman answered the door, and I explained our dilemma. I asked if the man I had seen was her husband and if he had noticed anything.

"No, it's just me here! I haven't seen anything!" I described the man and told her he had come from her yard. I thought he must be a neighbor or someone she knew. Perplexed, she said, "He came from here? I know everyone here. I even jog here. I have never seen the man you describe." She apologized for not being able to help, then noticed and motioned to a bag on the corner of her deck. It was my son's! I laughed heartily and said, "So, he was an Angel!" She responded, "Yes! An Angel! I have goose bumps all over me!" I replied, "Yes, me too!"

I believe that a human who had been watching my son leave and was concerned about the bag would have simply called our attention to the forgotten article before we left. I think he might have even waited on the dock with it for awhile to see if we returned. This was much more. It was a perfect lesson in faith and a perfect gift, filled with God's graces, for a fifteen-year-old who sometimes forgets.

Ardyth Fowler

Soup for the Soul

At 10:00 P.M. the week before Christmas, I left my office to go to the bank and get money for the coming week when I noticed a bag lady lying outside on a park bench with her shopping cart beside her. I had $20 in my pocket and I was debating whether to wake her to give her the money.

Just then another bag lady came up the walkway through the park. This second woman offered the one lying down some of the soup that she held in a paper cup. The second woman then went on to another bench where her own shopping cart was parked. I decided to give the money to her. When I approached this kind woman she asked that I leave her alone. I said, "I am not going to hurt you, I just want to give you this," and I handed her the $20 bill.

She said, "Oh, well that's kind of you, but I'm sure you need it more than I. You must have a family to take care of." I said, "Sure, but they're okay, we have all we need, and I just thought you could use this." She said,

"Well, I could pay you back on Monday. I might be getting some money on Monday, would that be okay?" I told her I didn't want it back, that this was a gift. She said, "Well, I will only take it if I can say a prayer for you." I told her that would be fine, and she said a prayer for me.

Over the past few years I have been approached so often by panhandlers that I have become less caring than I should be about these people who really could use some help. I don't know if there is any kind of miracle in this story, but if there is one, it is that it opened up my heart and gave me a whole new perspective on the lives of the people on the streets.

Michael Geier

The Society for the Spirit of Christmas

Four weeks before Christmas, I was laid off from my job. We were expecting the birth of our second child. All in all, things were not looking too bright for us: Christmas presents would not be possible this year.

About ten days before Christmas, a man I knew showed up on my doorstep. He handed me an envelope. I asked him, "What is this?" He said, "Merry Christmas."

I told him I could not accept or give Christmas presents this year because of the situation we were in. He told me to take the envelope. He then told me it was not a Christmas present. He went on to say I was doing him a favor. He wished me "Happy holiday!" gave me a hug, turned around, and left. Inside the mysterious envelope I was holding was $150 in cash and the following letter.

Dear Recipient:
You have been chosen by the "Society for the Spirit of Christmas" to receive this gift.

The only obligation to you is that someday when things get better for you, as they will, you pass a gift of Spirit along to someone who is going through a hard time in their life. It should be given to them in the same manner as this gift was given to you.

This idea started a long time ago when a person such as you, in a situation similar to yours, was given such a gift at Christmas. A person came to him and gave him a gift that was needed at that time. He was told that someday when things got better for him, and they would, it would be his obligation to pass this gift along in the same manner as it had been given to him. He was told he could not accept anything in return. He was also informed he was never to disclose to anyone from whom he had received this gift. By doing this, the true spirit of Christmas would continue to live on for eternity.

And now with your gift and the continuation of this tradition, you have been selected by the Society for the Spirit of Christmas to carry on and start a new line of this tradition.

You will know this because God will provide you with extra money during the Christmas season for you to distribute to another in need.

The Society for the Spirit of Christmas

Our faith renewed, my wife and I blessed "the Society," and looked forward to the day we would be on the giving end of the envelope.

Larry Wasielewski

An Exciting Christmas After All

I am a single mother with a young daughter. I work part-time at a children's shelter and full-time as a waitress at night. I was able to buy two little dolls for my daughter this past Christmas. That was all I could afford and still be able to pay our rent and other bills. Despite my limited income, Christmas miracles have been happening for us.

A waiter at work told me he had a spare artificial tree and offered to let us borrow it. We now have a tree! Over the years I've collected ornaments, and our tree looks lovely.

The director of the children's shelter, who has two girls—both much older than my daughter Shakkai—gave her two dolls, together with a little baby doll cradle that rocks and two little purses . . . the works!!!

Then my mom made a Christmas stocking for Shakkai that matches my childhood stocking!!!!

The only day I will have off for the holidays is Christmas, and thanks to a friend, I'll be cooking a turkey!

I asked God for a good Christmas, and by a series of little miracles that is exactly what we will have. All these wonderful miracles occurred after I gave a coat to a homeless man who did not have one and after I donated clothing to the shelter. It seems what we give out comes back to us, multiplied.

Megan Moon

The Living Christmas Tree

Several years ago, our church started a tradition of sponsoring one or more families in our county in addition to its regular community outreach at Christmas. One family sponsored that year was a single mother with two teenage sons in high school. She was working two jobs to make ends meet, and after injuring her leg in a fall, couldn't work her waitress job, which was her main source of income.

My mom and I went to the local store and bought the boys several pairs of underwear and socks as well as jeans and sweaters and a couple of fun items. The mother had told us she had bought a tree but had nothing to put on it. I was making beaded star ornaments, so I kicked up production and made a couple of dozen for them. Someone in the church bought lights and a topper for the tree. Another person else provided toiletries and cleaning items that food stamps don't cover. We collected enough food for them for a month as well as for Christmas dinner.

We had something for each member of the family.

We all wrapped and gathered everything into our cars for delivery. We pulled up to the modest little trailer with its immaculate yard. Before we could open the gate, the two boys came outside and started helping us unload everything as their mother stood in the door and cried with joy and gratitude. We took everything inside the house, which was spotless.

Her little Christmas tree was a cedar tree in a bucket. She planned to plant it outside after Christmas. The boys begged to be allowed to open one gift each while we were there, and they thanked us over and over again. We all decorated the tree and they cried for joy as we were leaving. Last year, our church received a $100 check in the mail from this woman and her sons, with a note thanking us for providing for them when their times were hard and asking us to give their donation to another family, just like we did for them. Her letter also mentioned that their little tree had grown and was thriving and had served them as a symbol of God's care and promise that things would get better. Simple things done for others can mean so much.

Katherine M. Aaron

May You Sleep Wrapped in the Arms of Angels

My mother loved children. She had lost four children at birth and was told she couldn't have any more babies. Much to her surprise, she had my brother when she was forty-two years old, and I was born the following year.

My mom and dad loved to give children love. As my brother and I grew up we always had a few extra children around; my parents took in fifty-four foster children over the years. Some children would stay a few days, some months, and others a few years.

My mom always used the same nightly routine to dispel fears for the foster children. She would open the closet doors and show the children that there were no monsters living there. Then she would say, "Look under your bed and see that there are no monsters under there either." Mom would always point out a few dust bunnies and ask the children to catch a few for her so she wouldn't have so much work to do. She would put us to bed with hugs and kisses and ask if we had left enough room for our Guardian Angels to snuggle in beside us and wrap their wings around us to protect us and keep us safe. We then said our prayers and went off to sleep.

I once asked Mom why she did this every night. She said, "Well, not all children have a safe home to be in like you do." She went on to say how some of the children wet the bed because they are afraid to get up and go to the bathroom. She wanted the children to feel safe and know nothing would hurt them. She illustrated this by showing them there was nothing in the closet or under the bed. My mother created the spirit of love and safety all year round, not just during the Christmas season. Maybe it is because of this loving woman that I have always seen Angels. To this day, as I go to sleep at night, I always leave room for my Angels to wrap their wings around me.

Atira Hatton

The Christmas Tree Angel

Yesterday was our day for Angels.

It was my son's third Christmas. In his short three years, we lost my grandfather—"Opa Ted"—and our very loyal Shetland sheep dog named Duchess. We thought about them as having moved on to another place and becoming our Guardian Angels. We had no doubt that our Angels were with us this Christmas.

Before putting my son to bed at the end of the day, we once again took in the beauty of our live and majestic eight-foot Grand Noble tree, with each ornament on it holding special memories of years past. It was topped with a beautiful Angel, bright with Christmas lights, given to us as a wedding present twelve years earlier. She has sat on top of and protected our tree for each of those twelve years. After tucking in my own little cherub, I came down the stairs and noticed the tree beginning to tilt. This didn't make sense to me, since no one was near it and it was securely screwed into the tree stand. Before I could reach it, it came crashing to the ground. Ornaments appeared broken and the water was emptying all over the carpet. Many of the ornaments were made of Belleek and were expensive and extremely fragile. My first reaction was anger and disappointment, and the words out of my mouth did not rhyme with "Angel."

Little did I know the words should have been, "Thank you, my dear Guardian Angels."

To my surprise, only one ornament had broken. As I reached to replace the treetop Angel, I noticed the first five inches of the top of the tree was brown and charred. Apparently, the wiring to the light was faulty and had begun to burn our tree. When my son came down to find out what had happened, he simply and matter-of-factly said, "I think Opa Ted and Duchess knocked it down." Had the tree not fallen, we would not have noticed it was burning until it was too late. Our Guardian Angels toppled our tree and saved our lives.

Angel Summer

Christmas Mail

The year I was seventeen, I was staying at my sister's home in California for the Christmas season. My sister and her family had gone to Long Beach to spend the holidays with her husband's family, and I was at their home alone. I was to put up the tree and put out the gifts for their children.

Although I had a job to occupy my time, I was all alone in the evenings, and I cried so hard, missing my mother, who was living with another of my sisters. I wanted to be with my mom during the holidays. My only brother had died right before Christmas eight years earlier, when he was seventeen, so it was always a very hard time of year for my mother. And here was Christmas, and I was in Sacramento, while Mom was in St. Louis. I didn't have the money for a phone call, and they could not pay for collect calls. I knew Mom would be missing both me and my brother; I was missing her, and I was filled with tears.

On Christmas Eve, I hurt so much, I decided to write a letter to my mother. I poured my heart out to her. I wanted her to get my letter as soon as possible, and I decided to try to get it into the mail before midnight. It was already 11:00 P.M. My boyfriend—who later became my husband—was visiting and he was upset watching me cry. He drove me to the post office so I could mail the letter.

The next morning, Mom was in the kitchen, preparing the Christmas dinner. She was thinking of me and crying. Everyone else was in the living room watching the holiday programs. Mom heard a sound at the back door. She opened it, and there was a young man standing with his left hand on the mailbox, which was hanging close to the back door. He was dressed in a dark blue suit, with a tie, and he was very clean cut. The suit looked the same as the one my brother had worn at his funeral. The young man looked so kind. My mother raised her apron to her eyes to dry the tears so she could see him, and to clear her throat so she could ask him what he was doing. When she looked again, there was no one there. She ran to the walkway, about ten feet, and looked—no one there. She ran to the street—no one there.

She went back, and before she went into the house, she decided to check to see why he had his hand on the mailbox, knowing there was no delivery of mail on Christmas Day. Inside, there was my letter, sent ten hours before from 2,300 miles away. There was no post-mark on the letter. It had been hand-delivered by my brother to ease her pain and to give his love to her. She called me the minute she finished reading my letter to ask me when I had mailed it. Mom told me the story on the phone, as I now tell you.

I know why this happened, and who made it happen. The Angels are helpers of God, and there is no need or desire so great that can't be handled with the help of the Angels.

June Becker

Christmas Present

In 1968 I was unmarried and pregnant. The baby's father had said he would marry me but then changed his mind and joined the Navy. Given the times, my family insisted I go to the home for unwed mothers and do the "right" thing. So away I went. In November I had a very healthy baby girl. Five days later I held her for the first time as the social workers were preparing to take her away.

My mother changed her mind after the baby was born and said I could bring the baby home. I told her it was too late. I had signed the papers, and my baby was going to be taken away. I received a letter from the baby's father the next day saying he was getting out of the Navy and coming home to marry me. "Please keep the baby," he wrote.

I was never told I could change my mind within a year's time. I thought I couldn't change my mind, and so I moved forward with my decision to give my baby up for adoption. I was so lost and in so much pain. But, even then, I believed everything happens as it is supposed to, so I didn't challenge this life decision.

The baby's father and I married in 1969 and had another beautiful baby girl—the absolute joy of my life! Her father and I separated when she was eight months old, and I raised her on my own with help from my parents. In 1989 I married a wonderful man who has the same birthday as my second daughter.

I had always had questions about my first child and wanted to know she was all right. And, I dreamed of the two girls meeting each other.

One day while I was working in the Recorder's Office, a young man came in to look up records on his biological parents. We started talking, and he told me I could look up my first daughter's birth certificate. I had always thought the adoptive parents changed the birth date, but I was wrong. I looked under her date of birth and wrote down all the girls born that day. There were twelve of them. I pulled out the reel of film and started checking. Number eleven was a match! I was so shocked when I finally had what I always wanted that I just couldn't move. I made a copy of her birth certificate and went home to share the information with my daughter and husband.

It turned out that my firstborn had been adopted by a very wonderful family in town . . . and had been living just five miles away from me for most of her life. My second daughter wanted to go over right away, but instead I called the adoptive father at work and talked to him. I explained who I was and why I was calling, and I asked if we could set up a meeting. He was also excited and said he would talk to his family that night and he would call me back. He called back at 9:00 P.M. and said come on over!

I was a mess!!! I was trying to find the "right" clothes, shoes, fix my hair. . . . My daughter and husband were going through the same jitters. Well, we finally got there and received the warmest welcome you can imagine! The mom had had one daughter of her own, and, after she was born, the doctors told her she couldn't have any more children. So they adopted my child. They then got pregnant again and had another baby.

My daughter is a beautiful, wonderful young woman who has had a great life!

Our meeting took place on December 5, 1990. We all had a great Christmas! I thank my God and my Angels every day for this wonderful Christmas miracle.

Yvonne E. Austin

Christmas Lights

L ast week, I had asked my daughter, Alexandra, to feed the dogs outside in the garage. Later that day I asked her if she had done it, and she said Yes. But I had a strong sense that I should go check on the dogs anyway. One of the dog's food bowls was still outside the garage, so I went over to the side door of the garage and opened it to get the bowl. When I bent over to pick up the bowl, there was a funny burning smell. I couldn't quite place it, but I got the bowl and shut the door.

Then as I stood up, I thought how odd that smell was and opened the door and looked around. I saw that the cord to our Christmas lights on the pine tree outside was nearly severed and was singed. The garage door had damaged it. The singed cord had been causing the burning smell. If I hadn't decided to check it, it doubtlessly would have soon started a fire.

What made me go to that door and double check? At the time, I said, "Thank you, God. You saved us." It seemed the only explanation to me then—and it still does now.

Kathy Cherroff

A Song of Christmas Love

The Angels came to me in the night with a song, a song of Christmas love.

One year on December 7, a Thursday night, I went out with my family to complete my Christmas shopping. The bookstore was one of our stops. I passed a table filled with books on Angels. I stopped to look through them, and a book called *Angelspeake* found its way under my arm with all my other purchases. The next morning, instead of wrapping all my Christmas treasures, I found myself curled up in my chair reading *Angelspeake.* Next thing I knew, the morning was gone and I'd read the book cover to cover. I went about my normal day, thinking of nothing more serious than what we would have for supper.

I didn't know how much my life would change in forty-eight hours. On Sunday morning around 2:00 A.M., I was awakened from a deep sleep with a song in my head. With the book fresh in my mind, I thought, "Could this be the Angels?" I decided to ask them questions. I had a small pad of paper and a pencil by my bed. I asked who my Guardian Angel was. The song continued. I tried to figure out what the music meant, when she spoke, "Don't talk, listen. Let your head clear." The Angels really were trying to talk to me! All of a sudden, I became frightened and began to pray. The next thing I heard was, "Way to go!"

I felt touched but not quite sure what purpose the incident served other than to let me know Angels are really here. The next morning around 3:00 A.M., I was again awakened to hear the song and the words, "Busy, too busy." I said again, "I'm trying to understand the song." "Love at Christmas," they responded. What could they want of me? "Love at Christmas" and "homeless" were their messages.

They didn't speak in complete sentences, just words, thoughts, pictures, and music. "Give Love on Christmas Day!" and again, "Give Love on Christmas Day!" then "homeless" and "We all have something to be thankful for" and "Thousands of streets are full of hungry people." I was getting the message! "So what do you think I can do about it?" I asked. "It's just fourteen days till

Christmas. I work retail and there are no hours left in the day."

The next morning I got up and read what I'd written the night before. My notes said, "Call Barbara." Barbara —the author of *Angelspeake*? I called directory assistance and much to my amazement, they gave me her number. I dialed, a woman answered, and I said, "Hello, my name is Mari. Are you Barbara Mark, the Barbara Mark who wrote *Angelspeake*?" She said, "Yes." At this point, the tears poured down my face. I proceeded to tell her of my encounter with the Angels, and we talked for an hour. I felt as though I was talking to family. She wanted to know what the Angels said. I told her they wanted me to feed the homeless on Christmas Day. I asked her how she thought I was to do this. She assured me the Angels would show me if I asked enough questions. She said at the end of our conversation, "So what are you going to do?" I answered, "What can I do? I have to find a way to feed the homeless."

Again the next night, at 2:45 A.M., I was awakened with "Pay attention." They did give me more information—about making stockings, filling them with food, oranges, candy canes, toothbrushes, and soap to help the homeless remember the joy of being children on Christmas morning. I asked how to make this happen and they said, "Ask for help."

I'm such an independent person that I'm not used to asking for help. But, I thought, this time I didn't see any other way. When I got up, I started cutting out stockings from my extra cache of fabric. The scissors were making blisters on my knuckles, and from nowhere came the words, "Don't you have oil?" I was sure I was on the right path even if I wasn't quite sure where I was going. I asked my colleagues at work for help. All of my coworkers eagerly agreed to help fill the empty socks, even when I told them it was an Angel project. Well, that seemed easy enough—now I just needed to finish cutting and sewing 200 stockings! I asked my husband to take some stockings to work and ask for help to fill them. He came back to me and asked me for more stockings to fill. I asked for help from people at the coffee shop where I stop on my way to work. They filled all their stockings and asked for more. I asked the chiropractor's office. They not only helped, but asked for more. I asked the people where I used to work. They helped, and then they wanted to do more. I was over-whelmed with the response.

Every night the Angels came to me. One night, exhausted, I asked, "Why do you wake me in the middle of the night?" "It's the only time you'll listen," was the reply. I realized then maybe I am "busy, too busy" to hear them during the day.

The food part of the project was going well, but just thinking about the toothbrushes and soap and other items made me worry that maybe this project was get-ting out of hand. I asked the Angels where I should go to get these items at a reasonable rate. "The hospital," was the reply. So, the next morning I called the hospital and asked to speak to someone in Supplies. A very nice man directed me to Dave from the supply company that sells toothbrushes to the hospital. When I finally reached Dave, I explained my project to him and asked about the toothbrushes. He said he would donate them. What a relief! I would get 200 toothbrushes at no charge.

Still on my mind was the soap. My husband said that in a city as large as Las Vegas, with all its hotels, getting soap shouldn't be a problem. He asked Arizona Charlies. They responded saying they needed a letter stating what our cause was. I wrote the letter, and the next day I had not only 200 bars of soap but lotion and shampoo as well! And, when I went back to pick up the toothbrushes, there were not the 200 I was expecting but more than 2,000! God was really watching over this project.

Finally, I wondered, how can we help these people help themselves? In my first conversation with Barbara, she gave me permission to use her book to help with the project. I copied the page that tells how the Angels will help you if you ask, reduced it to a 3 x 5 card, and attached one with a ribbon to each of the stockings.

Christmas morning, at 7:45, everyone met at our appointed spot. All of our helpers brought family members to assist. We loaded all the stockings into the back of a volunteer's truck and headed for the freeway underpasses of Las Vegas. Under some of them, homeless people were still asleep with blankets pulled over their heads, trying to keep out the cold. Near the road in old shopping carts were all their belongings in the world—nothing compared to what we call "nothing."

We quietly left the stockings, candy canes, and bottled water. I wished I could have been there when they woke up, but we had much more to do. I felt like Santa must feel, helping in the dark and quiet with the only reward coming from his own heart.

One large intersection had a lot of men living under it. We left stockings, candy canes, and quarters with a brief message that I shouted out to the men, now starting to stir: "Please call home. Someone does care and wants to know you're all right." One man shouted back, "God bless you!" As we left, we could see them starting to rise, excited by our visit. We stopped in the middle of the intersection to watch as one of the men came down and got the stockings and, like an excited child, started delivering them to his friends.

We got in our cars and headed off to our next stop. When we stopped at the traffic light, we saw a sight I will not forget as long as I live—all of the men were sitting up and poring through the contents of their stockings. We then headed downtown in search of a shanty village I had seen weeks before. I found the lot but it was vacant and clean. I guess someone didn't want them there. We pulled through St. Vincent's shelter, where there were just a few men. We were not sure if they worked there or if they were homeless. We came close to leaving when a few men approached us. We gave them stockings and quarters with the same "Please call home; someone cares" message.

I don't know where all the people suddenly came from. Three people had turned into thirty. A family crossed the street from nowhere—a father and mother and three little girls. A very young couple came up with a baby stroller. We gave them three stockings and two quarters. The woman turned to her husband and said, "We can call your mom now."

We still had places to go, but we dropped off extra supplies with the security guard at St. Vincent's and left five stockings next to the light pole for others who might walk by. We then headed off once again in search of those in need. As we were driving, we saw a man asleep on a bus bench. We pulled over, and quietly placed a stocking next to the sleeping man. Next, we headed to the Salvation Army kitchen. By now it was 10:15, and there were lots of people. We asked the guard's permission and gave him the blankets we had collected and 1,000 toothbrushes, and then we started to hand out stockings.

The people we saw—of all ages, all sizes, from all walks of life—found themselves homeless this Christmas for as many reasons as there are people. They were so thankful for the little we did. For most, it was all they received for Christmas. As we drove away, I watched a lonely older woman as she sat on the curb and started to remove the rubber band from her stocking and read the card about talking to your Angels. We touched so many lives that Christmas morning, and they touched us back.

In the car on our way back, my husband and I talked about next year. If we started right then, we thought, how many more stockings could we hand out next Christmas? And, we wondered, what can we do to help all year long? We talked about how easy it is in today's society to become homeless. Many people live week to week, month to month. It could happen to any of us. We need to be thankful for all that we have.

Christmas is a gift, a time to give love to all. Angels touch our world every day, not just at Christmas time. If you're willing to listen, they'll touch your life too. I'm sure they are not done yet.

Marilou F. Jackson

Editor's Note: Mari and her husband expanded their service to the homeless by serving breakfast in the park every Sunday morning. Mari returned to school and completed her degree in ministry, has received her ordination, and moved to Arizona where she and her husband still work with the homeless. When the Angels woke her up with their song of love, they really woke her up!

Christmas Lights for Joey

Our son, Joey, was born on Good Friday, March 28, 1997, and died at the moment of his birth. He was brought back to life, died two more times, and was resuscitated each time. We got to bring him home a few days later.

He was the greatest inspiration in my life and showed me what it really is to be a hero.

That fall I had a strong feeling we should put up our Christmas tree early, so we put it up on November 18. On November 21, Joey passed away, and a strand of lights on our Christmas tree went out. My husband and I were too filled with sorrow to fix the lights. We left the lights just the way they were.

Every day after Joey's death, I prayed to God that Joey would give me a sign he was with God and was safe and happy. I searched the Internet for comfort in stories, articles, poems, and for anything that would help ease the pain. One day I found "The Compassionate Friends." This group offers support for families who have lost children and also performs a Candle Lighting

Vigil on the second Sunday of December every year in remembrance of all the children who have passed over. They call it "National Children's Memorial Day."

People around the world light a candle at 7:00 P.M. local time on that day, in memory of all the children who have passed. This light encircles the Earth, creating a twenty-four-hour memorial. I felt a compelling need to tell everyone about the prayer vigil and this wonderful way to remember our children. In the thank you cards I sent out after Joey's funeral, I inserted a message to inform everyone of this special day and asked them all to share it with us in remembering Joey.

On December 13 at 7:00 P.M. my husband and I lit our candles. (We had more than twenty.) The instant we finished lighting our candles and said our prayer, the strand of lights on our Christmas tree came back on!

Our prayer to God was heard and answered, and it has given us hope and faith. I know in my heart Joey is safe and loved in heaven and that one day we will be reunited. Until then, Joey's memory will live forever in our hearts. He truly is our light.

Maria Strino

The New Believer

Just over a year ago my sister and I flew home to New Jersey to spend Christmas with our family. After spending a week with them, I was looking forward to returning home to California. The house was full of relatives, so the last night of my stay I slept on the living room floor and my sister slept in a nearby room. Very early in the morning I woke up but couldn't move. I knew where and who I was, and I could hear my sister packing. All of a sudden I had a pain and something that felt like a lump the size of an orange was in my chest. It was excruciating. There was something terribly wrong with my body.

I saw myself in a hospital bed (I was still aware that I was lying on the living room floor); a doctor looked at me and shook his head. He said to me, "I'm sorry there is nothing we can do now. You don't have long to live."

I felt the pain in my chest and thought I must be imagining what a doctor would be saying to me. I was not asleep. I was fully conscious, I couldn't move. I was scared half to death.

The next thing I knew, there was an Angel standing by my hospital bed acting like he was listening to someone behind him ready to pass a message on to me. He then looked at me and said, "We've decided to give you one more year to live, then we will make a decision as to whether you will stay longer, or die." All of a sudden the pain and lump in my chest was gone, and I was able to move. I was shaking and told my sister about the incident. I thought this must be a message from the other side telling me my time here was limited and to use it wisely. On the return flight home I couldn't stop thinking about it because it seemed so real.

When I arrived in California I called Paul, a friend of mine, to tell him I was back. He said, "I have some bad news for you." Mark, a mutual friend, "has just been admitted to the hospital. He went in to have a chronic cough checked, and they found a tumor the size of a baseball in his chest!" I was on my cell phone and was so stunned I had to stop my car. I knew instantly that it wasn't me the Angel was speaking about—it was Mark. I also knew Mark would live for one more year.

Mark went into remission, and one year later I went to New Jersey again to celebrate Christmas with my family. I had heard only a few days before my trip that Mark's cancer was almost gone, and he was not in any life-threatening situation. I flew back to California after Christmas and received a phone call almost exactly one year to the day from my vision saying that Mark was in the hospital with pneumonia, but he was going to be okay. A few days later Mark passed away.

I don't know why the Angel came to me, but he did, and I did give Mark the message from the Angel. 'One meeting with an Angel is all you need to know beyond any shadow of a doubt that they are here, watching over us.

David E. Banta

The Greatest Gift

Christmas Eve is a night most families of Polish descent celebrate the birth of Christ and express their love for the Christ child. Christmas Eve 1972 was a most memorable evening for our family.

In the early part of 1972, my husband, Tom, and I began seeking out adoption agencies in hope of adopting a child. The waiting lists were long and the children few. Time passed, but we didn't give up hope. Then one day, out of the blue, my mother received from her brother in Poland a letter that read, "A one-year-old baby boy has been abandoned in our local hospital. I have taken him home as a foster child because he would otherwise be sent to an orphanage, and he is too cute. Do you know anyone interested in adopting a baby boy?" Our prayers were answered—a baby in need of a family! We immediately sent a telegram saying we wanted the baby and would be in Poland in July. The next month was filled with trips to the State

Department, home studies from social services, passports, and waiting with anticipation.

We arrived in Poland in the summer of 1972. Tears of joy poured from our eyes as we met our relatives and our son-to-be. We fell in love with Greg immediately—big brown eyes, blonde hair, and a smile as warm as the sun. The next six weeks were filled with court proceedings and paperwork. Our free time was filled with long walks, ball playing, picnics, car rides, shopping, and picture taking.

After six weeks, our visas were ready to expire, and still the necessary paperwork was not completed. We had to leave Poland without Greg. We were overwhelmed with sadness. We left Greg with my mother's sister, who lives on a farm in Poland, while we waited, not knowing when or if he would make it to the United States. Once home, we made sure all the papers were in order on the American side of the adoption. Again we waited. The days grew into weeks and the weeks into months. Friends gently suggested that we not set our hopes too high. Our belief in God and Angels helped us through this period of time. Every morning we went to church and lit a candle to pray that we would have our son by Christmas.

The Christmas season was soon upon us. Advent, the time of expectation, the time Christians await the coming of the Lord, passed. Christmas Eve came. The day was busy. Everyone bought gifts for our new son, just in case. It was disappointing not having our baby with us to celebrate. We left for my parent's home, and as we were backing out of the driveway, the phone rang. I said, "Tom, I better answer it." I ran into the house. My mom was on the other end, and all she said was, "I'm leaving for the airport! Your son, Greg, is there with my brother!"

Can you imagine the screams of joy from the family when my mother drove up the driveway with our new son? That evening the family sat down to a good Polish dinner. Tom led the prayers: "Dear God, we want to thank you for bringing our child to us on the Eve of your birthday. God has always had his own mysterious way of doing things, and Christmas proves this better than any moment in history. We couldn't have received a more precious gift."

Greg was a delight from the day he arrived in our arms. He was full of energy, curiosity, and love. By the age of two he was already sitting in the high school baseball dugout with his dad, and by the time he was two and a half, he was sliding into first base. Greg was so outgoing and always brought laughter to those around him. We knew it was time to try and adopt again.

The next summer we returned to Poland. This time we went to a Catholic orphanage to see the children who needed loving homes. Greg was with us, and we spent the first day just playing with the children. The next day we had the difficult task of choosing a sister for Greg. This was so hard. If we were rich, we would have taken all four children who were up for adoption.

Finally my husband picked Renata because she looked like me. She was one year and three months old and very shy. We thought of changing her name, but Renata or Renee means "born again." How could we change her name? She was being born again. We were able to take Renee home with us immediately, but she hadn't been out of the orphanage and life outside was scary for her. It took lots of hugs, singing, and loving to turn the introverted Renee into the lively, loving, and super-extroverted Renee of today—truly a loving, enthusiastic young woman.

When we came home with Renee, I was tired. I thought it was the trip and the emotions of adoption, but it turned out that I was pregnant. God must work his miracles in mysterious ways. Seven months later Sheri Ann was born, and she brought more life and love into our household. Today, Greg is a baseball coach at a junior college, following his dad's career in baseball; Renee is teaching health and coaching tennis and softball at the local high school; and Sheri is teaching kindergarten. We have been blessed with these beautiful children, and they are now giving their gifts back to society.

Cathy Bergeron

Family Christmas

It took lots of footwork, quite a few Angels, and God's Divine Guidance to get me to where I am today. On December 12, I will have been clean and sober for ten years and off government aid for six years. The results of my previous actions had left my two children and me homeless.

Eight years ago, after being homeless for one month, I was living in student housing. It was an old military barracks where the owner (an Angel) would let students and a few others who were homeless live. My children were three and seven at that time. At Christmas I wanted to give to them a memorable celebration, but my income consisted of $295 in Aid for Dependent Children and food stamps; my rent, with utilities, came to $245 per month, leaving me with only $50 for gas, laundry, and supplies. I washed my clothes in the bathtub and hung them out on the guardrails or on hangers in the apartment. Needless to say, I could not afford Christmas gifts.

I knew I had to be creative. I was in school taking courses in computers and was able to work with Christmas graphics and print them out in black and white. I made a coloring book for each of the kids. I also started what is still a tradition in my family—making a wish book.

We saved old computer paper from the trash to create our wish books. The title on the books would read, "If I could give you anything, I would give you _____." The rest of the book would flow from whatever thought filled the blank. We went through old magazines and cut out pictures of what we wanted to give to the other person. Making paste from flour and water, we pasted the pictures on the empty pages. We added our own artwork with pencils, pen, and a few broken crayons. These books were wonderful. The first year I received a new car, a new house, and a new daddy (or should I say husband?) from my three-year-old daughter. My seven-year-old son gave me lots and lots of money, a meal fit for a queen, new clothes, and a puppy. I still have these precious books, and every year we make new ones.

Two years ago, the paper was fresh and bought from the store, not saved from the recycled can. We used brand new colors and paints, not broken little pieces. We had real glue, not flour and water. But the most special books were the first ones we made because we truly created them and gave from the heart, since that was all we had to give. Also two years ago, I had a new home, a new van, money in the bank, new clothes, and a puppy—and not just as pictures in wish books! I was married to a wonderful man who is truly sent from God, and we made a meal fit for royalty.

We now have a new tradition. We find families in need. We buy little things like socks, toothbrushes, hairbrushes, cologne, and food for Christmas dinner. We sneak up to the family's front door, leave the bags of goodies, and drive away. We have no intention of letting the family know who has given these gifts. We started with just one or two families, but last year we fed seventy-five people. I expect to feed at least 100 this year. Since the word has gotten out about what we are doing for Christmas dinner, others have stepped in to help.

The only things we paid for last year were the yams and one of the turkeys. This tradition has been going on for seven years.

You see, ten years ago I had a knock on my door at about 3:00 A.M. I was sleeping on the couch, as I always did, and when I heard the knock, I looked out my window. There were grocery bags in front of my door. Inside the bags were a few little gifts for the kids and food for a complete Christmas dinner. I had no way to cook this dinner, as our apartment did not have a kitchen, so I cooked it at a nonprofit organization that allowed me to use theirs. I invited a few people whom I knew had no other family except for us, and a few homeless people also showed up. I still use this kitchen to make Christmas dinner for large groups of people. You don't have to be homeless or penniless to join . . . loneliness is enough. Some of the folks are families who come for dinner and others are people who have chosen us as their family.

I have never considered myself an Angel for doing these things, but I see more and more how Angels have come into my life and how, in return, I have been encouraged to do things for others. I feel that I am giving back what was so freely given to me. I will never know who gave my children and me the gifts ten years ago, but the greatest gift of all to me has been the gift of giving.

Lydia R. Brown

The Perfect Christmas Tree

I had many challenges one Christmas. It was my first year without the physical presence of my two daughters. It would be my first Christmas together with my fiancé and my future stepson, Derek, who was seven. And, we were having financial challenges, leaving us without money to spend on even a tree. My heart ached to have at least a decorated tree and stockings at the chimney for Derek's visit with us; we still believed in the magic of the holidays.

On December 23 I took Derek and his friend to the fresh-cut tree tents located up and down our local streets. All the trees were too big and too much for my pocketbook. Sixty dollars was the least expensive tree I could locate on such short notice. But I didn't give up. The whole day I was racked with thoughts of "we can't afford a tree." But then I kept remembering the affirmations my minister had been teaching us, such as "Be willing to do whatever it takes." The day wore on and darkness came. I kept searching and decided to try out the local shops near the beach. I drove directly to Target, more desperate then ever. I walked into the garden area and saw three little pre-decorated fake trees and mentally decided that one of those would be fine. I asked the clerk for the prices, and he said, "I'm sorry, those trees are being donated to area charities, and they're not for sale."

Undaunted, I started to go inside and see what was available when I came across a small live tree lying on the floor. I picked it up and inspected it. "Perfect," I thought. "Perfect size, fresh and supple. This is the one." When I asked the clerk for the price, I was dumbstruck. I asked him to repeat the answer, and again he said, "It's free, just take it!" As humans do, I questioned this is in my mind. "Free . . . There must be something wrong with it." I inspected it again. It was still perfect, just the tree I was looking for, and the price was just perfect, too. I carried the tree out to my car, humbly thanking the clerk as I passed.

The next challenge was, "How will I pay to decorate it?" By then I was quite optimistic . . . it didn't matter. I knew it would be "perfect." I ran into Wal-Mart where I got decorations practically for nothing. It was the most wonderful tree I have ever had, and we had the most joyful Christmas.

Blessings abound!

Rebecca S. Sharp

The Christmas Rose

I once had a wonderful friend named Cheri. I loved her dearly, but about eighteen years ago our friendship ended over a misunderstanding. I really missed her after that. I saw her occasionally over the years, and sometimes would send a Christmas card, but it never worked out when I tried to get together with her.

We ran into each other this Christmas. She was in a hurry so we just said hello, and later I decided to send her a Christmas card. I hesitated to write more than my name on the card but after thinking about it, added, "I would really like to get together with you." It was Christmas week when I mailed the card, and I received a message on my answering machine the very next day. Her message said, "Thank you so much for the Christmas card, and, yes, I would love to get together with you, too." We never actually spoke directly, but through our exchange of messages, finally set a time and place to meet for dinner.

As I anticipated our meeting, I had mixed feelings. I was excited because connecting with her again was something I wanted, but I was also afraid we would only meet this once. I thought of bringing my friend one long-stemmed red rose as a token of everlasting friendship. I tossed this around in my head all week but then decided not to, thinking it might be too much, too soon. Strangely enough, as we sat down at the restaurant, my friend handed me a pin her daughter had made: a long-stemmed red rose. Her daughter makes rose pins in all colors but she chose to give me the red rose because she remembered how much I loved them. I could not believe it!

Dinner went very well. We had a wonderful time reminiscing about the old days and bringing each other up to the present. It was if time stood still, and I know we both felt the strong bond rekindle between us. We are older, but all the ingredients for a good friendship are still there. We have both grown spiritually and emotionally. I now believe we needed this separation to grow into the people we are today. Cheri says I am her favorite "Christmas Carol." We plan to get together again soon. Now that I expect miracles in my life, they happen. Especially the miracle of everlasting friendship.

Carol Goldberg

Family-to-Family

E very year at Christmas our Greek Orthodox Church does a Family-to-Family sharing program. It started out many years ago with only five families and a small number of church members participating. It's now grown to the point where over 200 families receive assistance in the form of twenty-four weeks of groceries, presents for all, and additional guidance and assistance where needed and welcomed. The firemen give us the toys from their "Toys for Tots" program, knowing they will be delivered where the need is greatest.

The best part of the program is that we don't drop these things off anonymously to some agency to disperse. That's where the "family-to-family" part comes in: Our families actually deliver personally to the families in need. It is quite an experience for our children to see other children become so excited over food, much less presents of toys or clothing. They begin to think a little beyond their own warm and cozy rooms. Rather than being frightened by the experience, their loving-ness begins to blossom. And every year seems to hold some surprise.

My favorite memory is the time we discovered an entire family of Russian immigrants: fifteen people aged six months to eighty-six years living in the garage of the house to which we were delivering for another family. They had nothing, and they weren't even on our list. Our parishioners had grown into the habit of returning to the church hall after their deliveries to see what else might happen and whether others might need assistance. This night, the group who found the garage came back, told the tale of the additional family, and everybody went swiftly to work. More toys were found, and funds were quickly raised to purchase additional food at the nearby supermarket. We went through the clothing collections and found something for everyone in the family, especially those who would be job hunting. Bibles and icons were collected.

A small group, including our priest and his wife, returned to the garage to deliver the supplies. The Russian family gathered and sang "Silent Night" in

Russian, and then our parishioners joined in, first in Greek and then English.

A little girl, probably five or so, gave her little Russian nesting doll as a gift to our priest. It was perhaps all she had in the world, but the family seemed unable to receive without also giving back. Everyone cried. This experience became one of the miracles of our giving program.

Brenda Ropoulos

New Year's Angels

It was New Year's Eve 1993, and I was driving home from work. I had not been on the highway more than a mile when suddenly the steering wheel of the car seemed to pull toward the left. I turned the wheel in the opposite direction to correct it and avoid hitting the concrete barrier dividing the highway. As I turned the wheel, something snapped and I lost complete control of the car. I tried to step on the brakes but they, too, had failed. I couldn't stop! Gaining speed, my car crossed over the right lane, then over the shoulder and down a steep embankment toward the railroad tracks.

I saw my life flash before my eyes. Everything and everyone who was important to me—from when I was a little girl to the present—was in that one flash of light. I thought that I was not going to live. I was so scared. "I am only twenty-three years old," I thought. All of a sudden, the car stopped, twenty-five feet before the railroad tracks. I looked around, unbelieving, to make sure that the car had really stopped. As soon as I realized that it was true, I grabbed my keys out of the ignition, got out of the car, and started walking up the steep hill to the highway to get help. As I looked back at the car, I was in awe of how it had suddenly stopped the way it did and that I was walking away from it with no injuries. Wondering how it happened and how it stopped, I realized God and his Angels were with me in this freak accident and there was no other explanation.

When I turned back toward the highway a car pulled up, stopped on the side of the road, and waited for me. When I got to the car, the couple inside told me that they had been traveling the opposite direction on the highway and saw me lose control. They turned around at the first place they could and drove to the site where my car went down the embankment. They were just coming from the city I was driving to and they offered me a ride home, although it was at least twenty miles out of their way. They never told me their names, just that they were married and that they were glad I was okay and home safe. They were Angels in human form.

Later, my family and I went back to look at the car to see what could have happened. Of course, this was New Year's Eve after hours, so there were no tow trucks available until the next day. At the site we gathered my belongings from the car and tried to figure out how it had stopped. There was no apparent answer . . . until I saw something intriguing. A vine was wrapped all the way around the front to the back of the car. It was a tiny, twist of branches, brown and dried. Nevertheless, it was wrapped all the way around the car. "Could this be the reason this car stopped?" I wondered to myself. I kept it to myself for a long time and considered myself blessed by God.

After the car was towed using a winch and chains to get it out of the embankment, the culprit was found to be a defective tie rod, causing the loss of control of the steering column. The men who winched the car out of the bottom of the embankment said that they could not see any reason for this car to have stopped the way it did, and that the tiny vine could not have stopped a car going fifty-five miles per hour down a steep hill. I know

how it did—it was God, helped by his miracle workers
we call Angels.

Julianne L. Behnke

143

Have You
"Pulled a Riekle" Lately?

Two days before Christmas, Howard turned to his friend Barbara and asked her if she would like to go to Cleveland-Hopkins Airport with him to "pull a Riekle." Although Barbara had never heard of such a thing, she was intrigued and curious about what Howard was suggesting, and she readily agreed.

As they drove, Howard explained what they were about to do. He told Barbara that he used to have a friend named Hal Riekle. He was a great guy, according to Howard, who had established a Christmas tradition. Hal would find several "someones" who could "use some upliftment" at Christmas and anonymously gift them with money or a gift certificate. Tragically, Hal Riekle was killed during the Gulf War. As a living memorial to him, Howard continued his friend's tradition each year by finding a number of "someones" on whom to bestow Hal Riekle's blessing.

Howard said he wanted to go to the airport this year because he had noticed that lately porters were not being well tipped, and he wanted Barbara to find a porter who could "use some upliftment." Barbara was to pick the porter who would receive one of this year's "Riekles" and was instructed to get the person's name so Howard could write it on a $100 gift certificate.

Delighted to go on this merry mission, Barbara left the car and surveyed the porters curbside, but none attracted her attention. She decided to go inside. It didn't take her long to spot him. She saw a youngish, African American man "with laughing eyes and a sweet soul" being used as if he were a piece of furniture. A thoughtless woman had propped a box up against the man—instead of choosing a countertop or chair—and was writing on the box as she pressed it against him. Barbara noted that the man took it all with good humor. Despite dismissive and what some might call obnoxious treatment by the woman, the porter warmly wished the woman a Merry Christmas as she peevishly departed for the gate.

Barbara had found her man, but she needed his name. She was hoping that once the box was removed, the man's name would be revealed on a badge or name tag. But no such luck. His name remained a mystery. So Barbara quickly concocted a ruse.

She approached the smiling porter asking if his name was Joe. He said no, his name was Bill and he really didn't know a porter named Joe. What airline did Joe work for, Bill inquired. Barbara quickly rattled off the name of an airline she knew to be at the opposite end of the airport, saying that Joe was holding a bag for a friend of hers and she needed to retrieve it. "Oh," Bill quickly explained, "that airline is all the way on the other side and Joe is undoubtedly there with the bag." Barbara wished Bill a Merry Christmas, and, as she began to turn away, he asked for her name. In this way he was able to respond in kind with a warm, "Merry Christmas, Barbara," as they parted company.

Barbara's heart soared with the thrill of finding such a wonderful man, and she could hardly wait to get to the car to tell Howard who the recipient would be. And although Howard had hoped for both a first and last name to put on the gift certificate, he took out his pen and wrote "Bill" for the recipient's name.

Next it was Howard's turn to bound out of the car on a mission. Barbara had described Bill to him and told Howard approximately where to look for Bill inside the airport. Spotting him easily, Howard strode up to the porter and inquired, "Is your name Bill?" The porter smiled back at Howard and said, Well, yes it was. Howard then proceeded to tell the porter that he worked for a man named Hal Riekle and that Hal had been at the airport about six weeks ago loaded down with many bags. Howard continued the tale by saying that Hal had felt badly because he had not had money with him at the time for a tip. Howard announced that he had been sent by his employer to give Bill this gift certificate signed by Hal Riekle to make up for the nonexistent tip, and to thank him for being so kind and helpful. Bill's eyes lit up even brighter than normal; he was obviously stunned and thrilled. "Oh my goodness," the porter said, "I don't remember the man, but I remember the bags!" The men parted with warm wishes, and Howard disappeared into the crowd.

Imagine the positive impact this "Riekle" had not only on Bill, Howard, and Barbara, but on all the other porters Bill told his story to. It's not too great a stretch to imagine many porters being inspired to hand out extra smiles and good wishes to travelers—travelers who might have also been inspired to pass the good cheer along. It doesn't take much to make a positive impact on our world—spreading good cheer in an ever-expanding ripple effect. Imagine the difference in our world if each one of us "pulled a Riekle" just once during the year. After all, any of us can "pull a Riekle" at any time, during any season. Imagine the power of your Riekle, and my Riekle and your next door neighbor's Riekle to literally transform the world. As the optimistic little tyke in the movie *Angels in the Outfield* repeatedly said with hope in his eyes, "It could happen."

Come to think of it, Hal Riekle will undoubtedly get an angelic kick out of it as well!

Jill H. Lawrence

Getting Ready for Santa

It was Christmas Eve, and my daughter was just four years old. After we had enjoyed some special holiday cider and cookies, it was time for my daughter to go to bed. She knew that for Santa to come she had to be asleep, but that didn't keep her from chattering a mile a minute about all of the wonderful things she was enjoying about Christmas. Finally, her eyes closed and she went to sleep.

My next door neighbors had invited me over to their apartment that evening. I felt comfortable about joining the festivities they had planned since it would be easy to check on my daughter. However, while I was there enjoying the party an intense urge hit me to go home. I immediately left and went back to my apartment.

Upon opening the door an unexpected sight greeted my eyes. In the middle of stacks of torn Christmas wrapping paper, tissues, and holiday ribbons my daughter looked up at me, beaming, "Look Mommy! Santa was here!" I was speechless. All I could come up with was, "Wow!"

So it was Christmas, celebrated very late that Christmas Eve instead of early morning. Her spontaneity and joy created a whole new experience. Kids have a way of doing that, don't they?

Donna Seebo

Angel Lights

Before Christmas, my wife and I were driving through our neighborhood when we both said in unison, "Did you see THE Angel?" Well, obviously, we both did!

Some neighbors had put Christmas lights up on a tree in front of their house. From the front of the house the lights were nothing unusual, just a long strand of lights in a random oval shape. But, when driving toward it from a few hundred feet down the road, the side view was a perfect Angel! The wings pointed toward the road and she was reaching toward the house. Amazing—these were randomly placed lights.

My wife had recently lost her brother and was having difficulty accepting it. She had immersed herself in Angel lore, and seeing the Angel in the lights helped strengthen her. Soon after, we took our seven-year-old to see the lights. He, like his mother, really missed his uncle, and he got so excited and happy to see what looked like an Angel.

When I asked the people who lived there if they knew what their Christmas lights had become, they said that lots of people had mentioned the Angel in the lights. What a wonderful Christmas present for all of us!

Rich Greffrath

The Spirit of Christmas

Each Christmas holiday season, shoppers descend on downtown Seattle determined to fill their shopping bags with carefully selected gifts for everyone on their list. I do something a little different. I set out for downtown Seattle with a shopping bag too, only at the beginning of the day, mine is full and by the end of the day it's empty.

You see, I give away presents to the homeless on the street. I start in November collecting things for the homeless and purchasing items every time I go to the store. I purchase small items that can be kept in a bag or pocket: nail clippers, shampoo, perfume, a pocketknife, razors, socks, gloves, and hats. I also try to find inexpensive special items like jewelry. I sort everything into piles and wrap them in packets marked for women, men, and children and head off for downtown.

I love giving my gifts and talking to the people. Some have said that this is the first present that they have had in years—others have cried with joy. When I return home with my empty bag my heart is full of love, and I know that I have had a successful day.

Once I gave a women's package to a man and didn't realize it for a while. I hurried back to make an exchange, and he said he had already opened it. He said he really wanted to keep it because he would rewrap it and give it to his wife for Christmas.

I encourage everyone to keep a shopping bag in their closet year-round and to purchase one item each time they go to the store. When the bag gets full, all they have to do is drop it off at a shelter for the homeless. An easy way to make a difference.

Joy J. Golliver

My Christmas Angels

I was nineteen and living at home with my parents. I was working two jobs, had a little extra money, and wanted to do something special for Christmas. My parents worked hard to provide for their six children, and although at times it was a struggle they always found it in their hearts to share what little they had with others. Seeing the joy they brought to people, I wanted to do the same. I called the social service agency in our town and they gave me the name of a family who needed assistance.

My parents and I went to their home and found not just one family, but five families living in one house! I can still feel the tugging at my heart when I saw all these children and wondered how was I ever going to give to only one of the families and not the others.

My parents and I pulled together and did some creative shopping—trying not to leave anyone out. There were four girls who were about my size, and I decided to part with winter coats that I had in my closet and buy them gloves, scarves, and hats to match. We brought more than a carload of gifts, from lamps to an area rug to groceries. The families' gratitude when we delivered the gifts on Christmas Eve was unbelievable.

Then, on Christmas morning, we heard a knock on our door. There were the four girls with the coats and matching scarves—they looked like little Angels. Only one was able to communicate in English, and she told us their families were grateful for all we had given to them, and they had a present for us. She then handed me two hand-embroidered pillowcases and tamales that they had made for us that morning. I don't know how they ever were able to find our house, nor did I think they knew our names. That was the year I came to realize the true meaning of Christmas Angels.

Susan C. DeMerit

Cabbage Patch Christmas

It was December 1983 and everyone was going crazy for Cabbage Patch dolls. The doll manufacturers couldn't make them fast enough. The dolls were impossible to find in stores. If you were lucky to find one in a store, you took your life in your hands trying to get it. Of course, that's what my daughters wanted for Christmas. I realized it was going to take a miracle to find them their Christmas wish dolls.

The closer it got to Christmas, the more I began to worry. The night before Christmas Eve, I still didn't have the dolls they wanted for Christmas. It looked like my children's faith in Santa would be destroyed. What would I tell them?

As I looked out the window, I noticed it had started to snow, the first of the season. It looked beautiful, sparkling as it fell. I thought it even looked magical. As I watched the snow I began to pray, "Dear God, please don't let my little girls be disappointed. If they don't get the dolls they may never believe in Santa again. They are too little to lose their faith in Christmas."

The next morning, Christmas Eve day, my husband left early to run some errands. The toy store in town had just opened, and he thought he would take a chance and check for the dolls. Of course, everyone was running to the doll section. On the shelf were fifty Cabbage Patch dolls. Everyone was grabbing for them, and my husband was able to reach down and pick one up. There was a limit of one per customer.

He was so excited that he came right home to tell me he had bought one. I was excited too. "Thank you, God," I thought to myself. Then, as happy as I was, I realized my problems were not completely solved: I had one doll and two little girls. How could I choose which of my daughters would get this one? Then the phone rang: it was my close friend calling to ask if I still needed a doll. Her neighbor's son worked in a toy store and he called her to find out if she knew anyone who wanted a Cabbage Patch doll.

Of course I exclaimed, "Yes!"

All I could do was give thanks to God for sending us a few Angels to orchestrate everything to happen the way it did. He answered a mother's prayer on Christmas Eve and made two little girls very happy on Christmas Day. The Cabbage Patch dolls we received were boy dolls. My daughter Michele named her doll Matthew, which means "Gift from God."

Christmas is a time for miracles, and God can make them happen, no matter how big or how small.

Sandy Mansfield

The Gift of Giving

My Aunt Mary was a nun. When I was a child, each year she would ask my parents to help her raise money and buy gifts for all the underprivileged children it was her privilege to serve. My parents would buy toys and get donations from family and friends, and, as it got closer to Christmas, they would deliver these goodies to the children.

One Christmas, my parents had bought for me every toy that was on my Christmas wish list. My toys were in the trunk of my parents' car, but since that's where the toys being donated were also kept all the toys got mixed up together. By the time my parents realized what had happened, all of my toys had been given away! And, since it was already Christmas Eve, my parents had no time to replace my toys before Christmas.

My greatest gift came that year when I learned the value of giving rather than receiving. Although it was a difficult lesson, I was blessed and happy to share my overabundance with children who had so little.

My loving and generous family replaced those toys with a lesson for life. A lesson that taught me to feel blessed and taught me to share my gifts with those who need them most.

Mary C. McGrann

An Angel in Disguise!

In early November I called my chiropractor, Dr. Trish, whom I hadn't seen in many months. Much to my surprise, she said she had also planned to call me that same day. In her limited spare time, she had reread all my X-rays taken since 1985, and they showed that I had a progression of problems: osteoporosis and degenerative disk disease, as well as scoliosis and arthritis.

During the call she also told me that she and her family and her seven siblings weren't giving presents to each other this Christmas. Instead, they were planning to collect the money they would have spent on gifts and give that money to a family in need. They had chosen our family as the one to receive the money! She said she had seen my family go from being a healthy young couple to where we are now, with children, and she admired our courage and spirit. I was really thrilled, but after Thanksgiving came and went and she didn't call me back, I figured that they had found someone else who had a greater need than we did.

A few days after Thanksgiving, Dr. Trish knocked on my door and handed me a card and a gift-wrapped package about the size of a magazine. She had to get back to work so she left quickly before I could open it. I opened the card first, and it said, "Merry Christmas to your family . . . from some folks who care." I opened the package, and to my surprise there was a manila envelope with $850 in cash! Thanks to those "folks who care," even though we were going through hard times, we had Christmas at our house that year.

She was truly our Angel in disguise, helping us in a time of need.

Trish D'Abate

Santa's Visit

I teach handicapped and terminally ill children, and every year at Christmas my co-teacher and I take them to the mall to see Santa. This holiday season we arrived in the mall around 10:00 A.M., only to find that Santa would not be arriving for another hour. We then decided to take the twenty-one children into F.A.O. Schwartz, which we had originally planned to do after seeing Santa. If you have ever taken twenty-one handicapped children into a toy store for an hour you know what the scene was like. "Put that down. . . . Be careful . . . . I'm sorry ma'am, he didn't mean to run over your small child with his wheelchair. . . . "

At 10:45 I started lining the children up to see Santa. He came and as usual was wonderful—the same gentleman every year who has always been so patient and kind. As I was taking a picture of each child on Santa's lap my co-teacher came out of the store in tears. I thought something had happened to one of the children.

Something had—but it was so wonderful it was a Christmas miracle. It seems a man who was in the store shopping had been watching us with the children. This good Samaritan gave the manager of the store $500 for us to spend on things for the children! She went back in to thank the man and I continued to take the children's pictures, crying all the while.

The staff at the toy store was fantastic and helpful. We got to buy so many games, books, puzzles, and toys. Then the manager asked me if I could use the Brio train set that they keep set up. It seems it was "obsolete" because they were coming out with a new one for display. He not only gave us the display but all the trains and special accessories to go with it! One of my children wanted a little aquarium that cost $40, and they only charged me $20! The manager then gave me his card and said we should call him next September; they wanted to do a fund-raiser for us! The assistant manager was even going to come out to the school and show the children how to use the music keyboard and floor keyboard, like the one in the movie *Big*.

I was just overwhelmed by the kindness and generosity from so many people. One of my children looked at me and said, "It's just like being touched by an Angel!" I could not agree more.

Phyllis Driggers

Christmas Cookies

After a flurry of last minute Christmas shopping, I was trying to leave a very crowded parking lot. As I was waiting to turn, I saw a gentlemen with a sign up over his face reading, "Merry Christmas . . . please spare some food!" All I could see were his eyes showing over the top of his sign. A little voice inside me said, "Stop . . . turn around . . . go back."

I went around the block and parked my car. In the back seat I had several plates of cookies that I had made for friends. Taking one of the plates I walked up to him and said, "Merry Christmas." He responded, "Bless you."

As I turned away I had this heartfelt smile on my face and truly felt like an Angel. When I drove back by him, he was eating a cookie and looked at me with tears in his eyes. I was so touched. My heart was overflowing with the knowledge that I had touched someone's life.

Sue Morton

A Santa Cover-up

My brother Paul is one of the kindest people I know. Christmas is his favorite time of year. The joy of giving seems to envelop him; his spirit literally beams as he shares his joy with others. You would never guess that Paul is Jewish.

Some years ago, two of Paul's best friends gave him a dime-store Santa suit. From the moment he possessed it, it possessed him. Every Christmas Eve, he would put on the suit and the cotton beard and the plastic belt and he would become transformed into Santa Claus.

The first few Christmases he visited the children's ward in various hospitals, handing out candy canes and feeling the elation of children who knew that Santa had found them—even in the darkest of places. He rang his giant set of bells and "Ho Ho Ho'd" his way through the hallways letting all know that bright eyes and a smile would be expected when he arrived in their rooms. After his hospital adventures, he would return home exhausted, his voice gone, but with a true contentment few could possibly know—unless they've actually put on a Santa suit themselves.

One year, Paul added an unwed mother's shelter to his list of places to visit. Children would sit upon his lap telling "Santa" what they hoped would be under the Christmas tree, and then posed for a picture as an everlasting moment of their visit with Saint Nick.

The following Christmas he visited all of his friends who had small children. They would plan it so the children would catch him leaving gifts in their stockings. He'd exchange a few words in his deepest Santa voice, but only a few precious words so as not to give them an inkling they were meeting anyone but the genuine article. To this day some of those kids still believe.

And then last Christmas a miracle happened. Paul was driving home from his last delivery, looking forward to spending Christmas Eve curled up in bed with his dogs, watching *It's A Wonderful Life*. The streets were as quiet. A choir was singing on the radio. As he came to a stoplight, he noticed a homeless person sleeping on a bench under a few sheets of newspaper.

As Paul drove past this person, he remembered his

Santa sack in the trunk of the car, stuffed full of blankets to make it look full. He turned his car around, pulled over, removed the crumbled newspapers from the sleeping man, and replaced them with a nice warm blanket.

Can you imagine walking by and seeing Santa carefully covering up a sleeping man on a bench? Can you imagine an onlooker telling the new blanket owner who had covered him? Paul could only imagine the look on the man's face when he woke up Christmas morning under a brand new blanket. He laughed all the way home.

My brother Paul believes, "There are three ages of a man—when he believes in Santa Claus, when he doesn't believe in Santa Claus, and when he *is* Santa Claus."

Missy Smock

Afterword

by G. W. Hardin, co-author of
On the Wings of Heaven and *The Messengers*

Two thousand years ago, angels announcing the birth of the Messiah appeared to shepherds. Why shepherds? Why not kings or holy men, dowagers or priestesses? What is it about angels that attracts them to the most common of humanity? And what is so important about everyday people that angels find it necessary to show up in our lives? Frankly, it's because we're so wonderful. Truly. If the stories in this book do nothing else, they remind us of the stunning power of recognizing the Divine in the most simple, acknowledging our blessings, showering our blessings on life around us. Two thousand years ago the angels gave a message to shepherds: Peace on earth. And once again that same message echoes through the chambers of our collective hearts as the angels foretell once again of a world of peace.

Who can deny the changes flowing across our world? As before, we have the choice to see those changes as catastrophic or monumental. To those in power, the birth of the Christchild loomed as a threat; to shepherds, it was a blessing for the ages. Because of my writings, doors have opened that allow me to visit and discover some of the most spiritually gifted people on our planet. And I am here to tell you what they tell me: Once again the promise of peace shall be given to humanity. And once again, we will have the choice of accepting that gift in the living of our lives or rejecting it through the choices we make around, through, and within ourselves. Change has never come through governments or nations, princes or generals. No, change has always come through grassroots movements. It is the shepherds of the world, not the powers of the world, that foster and spread change. What war has ever changed a mind? What nation has ever forced another into truth? Wars have never solved problems. They inevitably cause new ones. Throughout history, real change has come from and through individuals. A small babe brought more change to this world than all the legions of Rome. And the angels fully understood that the truest way to ensure the coming changes would be through simple shepherds.

Now, like never before, we posses the opportunity to manifest a New Christmas, a new birth of Christ Consciousness. And like the shepherds, our simple everyday world is the key to this monumental change, this new chance at world peace. And how? you might ask. Quite simple, really. The very pages of this book hold the answer. The truths brought forth by these stories of human experience tell us that each of us holds memories or the capacity of remembering what it takes to foster peace, to live peace. You see, it's not enough to talk about peace. It's not enough to wish for peace. Peace must be lived one life at a time. And you, dear reader, are that one important single life. To recognize the truth in this idea is the first step. The second step is to do what the people who've shared these stories have done: Share your story, your experience of peace. The third step is to go beyond the sharing of a single Christmas event, to either foster or create a New Christmas event. And one of the best ways of manifesting such events is to reenact them, pass them on. Many in these little stories have simply passed on the goodness, the caring, or the peace-making once given to them. And now that they have passed on their New Christmas event to you, why not discover the real power in this book by passing the event that meant the most to you on to another. Too simple? That's what makes it so powerful.

Once one of us furthers an act of kindness, mercy, or peacegiving by passing it on, we send forth a spark that eventually blazes into a bonfire in the common heart of humanity. The light we initiate continues ever higher like a funeral pyre releasing us from a deathlike trance, allowing us to see the real message of Christmas: We are the peace on earth. We are the echoes of goodwill harmonizing with the choirs of angels, singing forth the New Christmas.

May this New Christmas be yours. Pass it on.

With love from my heart to yours.
G. W. Hardin

Acknowledgments

I WOULD LIKE to thank the following people, who have been an inspiration not only to me, but to many others:

My mother, Ellen, my hubby, Howard, and our daughter, Ariel, for their humor and support, which keep me going on this hectic, fun-filled journey called life.

J.J. and Jo and all their wonderful children.

Atira Hatton, for her continued support, guidance, and love. The Angel work you do is a marvel.

Earth Angel Michael Baumann, who volunteered to create and maintain Angelscribe.com. Michael's wisdom and skills allow miracles to flow into more homes and hearts.

Steve Koda, a powerful man whose heart leads him forward on all his endeavors. He uplifts and touches all those around him.

Earth Angels Patrick and Elizabeth Murphy. That they make the world shine brighter through their very presence is an understatement.

Jill Lawrence of Wisdom Radio, for giving wings to the air waves, and for making us laugh while sharing Angels with the world.

The unseen and much appreciated volunteers who support the *Angels and Miracles Good-News-Letter:* Kathy Adams, Bennie Campbell, James Davis, Jackson Hanks, Jenny Hansell, Ron Hays, Warren Hendrickson, and Brenda Ropoulos.

The people on the Angels and Miracles Prayer Team, which sprang to action from the newsletter: Prayer Team Coordinators Cynthia Morse and Judy Newman-Podlesny and all the Earth Angels who support them and volunteer their time to pray for all the people who request support. They are truly God's heart in action. An extra hug goes to Cynthia, who also gifted us with her editing skills for this book.

Authors Doreen Virtue, Marianne Williamson, Arielle Ford, John Harricharan, Jackie Waldman, Nick

Bunick, and Gary Hardin. Their open hearts and support are a blessing to many.

Syd Simard, for the hundreds of ways he supports the Angels' work, and Frances Rossi, Haldean Windsor, Lisa Thompkins, and Randy Powell for the fun memories.

Carmelina Cutajar, Larry Marcy, Marie Rhodes, Haizen Paige, Muriel Will, Sherry Hudson, Nickie Van Den Bosch, Anne Caldwell, Dana Walker, and Cynthia Fitzgerald. Earth Angels are everywhere, and these are some extra special ones.

In memory of Dr. Robert E. Parrish, who was always a healer of the spirit. We will see you in the stars.

PAX-TV and Wisdom Radio for the good works they are sharing with the world to uplift us: Check them out at: **www.paxtv.com** and **www.wisdomradio.com.**

Jeff Rogers, for forwarding my newsletters on to Conari Press. Jeff was the magical link between the work I was doing and Conari Press and you!

The hardworking staff at Conari Press, who created this heartfelt book for you and your friends and family to enjoy: Mary Jane, Will, Leslie, Pam, Heather, Sharon,

Rosie, Annette, Teresa, Jenny, Claudia, Suzanne, Everton, and Mignon. And a special thanks to Brenda Knight, for "discovering" me on the Internet and realizing that the spirit behind my newsletters could be transformed into wonder-filled books. . . . You were right!

And thank you to all the folks who lovingly contributed their stories to create the spirit of *A Christmas Filled with Miracles* for you and your loved ones to enjoy this holiday.

Contributors

Katherine M. Aaron

Linda Adler

Lilas (Hanebuth) Asher

Yvonne E. Austin

David E. Banta

Anne Bayley

June Becker

Julianne L. Behnke

Cathy Bergeron

Lydia R. Brown

Susan Caldwell

Kathy Cherroff

Katie Cole

Trish D'Abate

Susan C. DeMerit

Eddie deRoulet

Phyllis Driggers

Charles (Skip) F. Englehart

Ardyth Fowler

Michael Geier

Carol Goldberg

Joy J. Golliver

Rich Greffrath

Atira Hatton

Marilou F. Jackson

Kathe Kenny

Mary King

Jeanne Kvarda

Jill H. Lawrence

Sandy Mansfield

Sister Mary Julia, O.S.B.
Aynne McAvoy
Mary C. McGrann
Phyllis McLaughlin
Megan Moon
Sue Morton
Patrick J. Murphy
Robert E. Parrish, Ph.D.
Marie Rhodes
Brenda Ropoulos

Frances S. Rossi
Donna Seebo
Rebecca S. Sharp
Myrna L. Smith
Missy Smock
Maria Strino
Angel Summer
Betty Tisdale
Larry Wasielewski
Dale S. Westerberg

Do You Have a Miracle to Share?

TO SHARE A miracle story is to be a teacher of the soul. Miracle stories offer hope and inspiration and motivate people to open their hearts and grow.

The first true miracle Christmas story I heard was the one my grandmother published in her Vancouver newspaper, the *Elder Statesman*. It was told to her by one of her good friends. His miracle happened during the war when he was a prisoner. One of his fellow prisoners was lucky enough to work in the kitchen, and from time to time he would sneak food back to the barracks for them—under penalty of death. On Christmas Eve this brave prisoner concealed a sack of rice and carried it from the kitchen to the barracks. When he was back amongst his mates, he thought they would be enthusiastic, but instead what he saw were ashen faces and gaping mouths. Unbeknownst to him, as he had left the kitchen the sack of rice had caught on a nail, and had laid a perfect trail of rice to their cabin. From Christmas Eve to Christmas morning was a long night as they waited for the morning's punishment. But Christmas morning was greeted by one of the men looking out the window and shouting in great enthusiasm.

It had snowed during the night, and the rice had been covered by freshly fallen snow! When the prisoners were allowed out into the snow by their guards, they played soccer to kick, mix, and bury the rice in the resulting mud, thus saving their lives.

Miracles are often acts of kindness wrapped in love, which give us hope and inspiration. The more you open your hearts and share with the intention of love, the more wonders manifest in your life. To become a virtual miracle magnet, every morning, for three months, ask to be a Divine Vehicle for the energy of God/the Angels/Spirit to work through you for the good of everyone. This simple technique has great power. And when your miracles manifest, write to me so we can share them with the world.

Please write to me:

> Mary Ellen Angelscribe
> P.O. Box 1074
> Cottage Grove, Oregon 97424
>
> www.angelscribe.com

About the Author

Michael Sergasson

Mary Ellen lives in the world of Angels and Miracles.
She is the creator of the *Angels and Miracles Good-News-Letter* on the Internet, and author of the bestselling
book, *Expect Miracles*. She is also a commentator for
Wisdom Radio's WholeNEWS. Mary Ellen Angelscribe is
a Canadian living in Cottage Grove, Oregon, with her
daughter, Ariel, husband, Howard, pound pets, and, of
course, her Angels.

To Our Readers

ONARI PRESS publishes books on topics ranging from spirituality, personal growth, and relationships to women's issues, parenting, and social issues. Our mission is to publish quality books that will make a difference in people's lives—how we feel about ourselves and how we relate to one another. We value integrity, compassion, and receptivity, both in the books we publish and in the way we do business.

As a member of the community, we sponsor the Random Acts of Kindness™ Foundation, the guiding force behind Random Acts of Kindness™ Week. We donate our damaged books to nonprofit organizations, dedicate a portion of our proceeds from certain books to charitable causes, and continually look for new ways to use natural resources as wisely as possible.

Our readers are our most important resource, and we value your input, suggestions, and ideas about what you would like to see published. Please feel free to contact us, to request our latest book catalog, or to be added to our mailing list.

2550 Ninth Street, Suite 101
Berkeley, California 94710-2551
800-685-9595 • 510-649-7175
fax: 510-649-7190 • e-mail: conari@conari.com
www.conari.com